Confident Kids

'Although childhood fears and phobias have been researched for many years, it is surprising that so little has been written for children and parents in the area. This manual represents a significant step towards overcoming this deficiency, and should be very helpful to parents (or children) working towards the resolution of maladaptive fears.'

Dr Neville King, Faculty of Education, Monash University

'This is the book which every parent with an anxious child needs to have. Its fun illustrations and simple, easy-to-follow strategies for handling fear reassure children that they aren't the only kids who feel scared and that there are things that they can do to become less afraid and more confident.'

Helen McGrath, Psychologist and author

'Supportive, informative and humorous — a book which will empower children to deal with their fears in a relaxed and constructive way. *Confident Kids* is a practical and informative guide which will give parents confidence in dealing with their child's fears. A great resource.'

Jenny Rickard, Psychologist and author

'I believe that this is an important contribution to self-help resources for parents wishing to take an active approach to their children's fears. It contains much useful information and practical suggestions for activities that will provide a firm basis for helping children through the common problems of fear.'

Rob Gordon, Consultant Psychologist, Royal Children's Hospital, Melbourne

Confident Kids

Helping Your Child Cope with Fear

FEAR BUSTER

DR JANET HALL

With cartoons by Neil Matterson

A LOTHIAN BOOK

A Lothian Book

Thomas C. Lothian Pty Ltd
11 Munro Street, Port Melbourne, Victoria 3207

First published 1993
Reprinted 1993
Copyright © Janet Hall 1993

National Library of Australia
Cataloguing-in-publication data:

Hall, Janet.
   Confident kids: helping your child cope with fear.

   ISBN 0 85091 577 5.

   1. Fear in children. 2. Parent and child. I. Title.

155.41246

Cover design by The Small Back Room
Text design by Lynne Tracey
Illustrations by Neil Matterson
Typeset in Cheltenham by Bookset Pty Ltd
Printed in Australia by Griffin Paperbacks

Foreword

Growing up for children is a complex process as they come to terms with the world around them. Much can be frightening to them because they are yet to develop the knowledge and thought processes to deal with new experiences to which they are exposed. If they do not receive help from their parents and other adults whom they love and feel confident with, then these new experiences can become very frightening. Regrettably at times their fears are reinforced by inappropriate responses from adults, particularly if the experience is accompanied by pain or discomfort.

If these fears are allowed to go unchecked, they can develop into distressing phobias. The child may become much troubled by frightening nightmares.

Parents need to recognise that fears are a normal part of the child's development and that the child must be helped to deal with them. This book provides a very practical approach. Having a separate section for children is particularly helpful. The parents' section correctly recognises that some fears are appropriate but then shows them what to do with fears that are inappropriate. The child's section allows it to be written in a way that is understandable by children.

We need to help our children to develop into confident adults with an appropriate response to the happenings around us. If this book helps in this process, it will serve a very valuable function.

PETER D. PHELAN
University of Melbourne
Stevenson Professor and Chairman
Department of Paediatrics
Royal Children's Hospital

Acknowledgements

Thank you to all the people who contributed to the creation of this book and especially to Jill Branagan, 'Problem-Buster' supreme. Special thanks, too, to my children, Pamela and Robin, who gave invaluable feedback from the kids' point of view.

Thank you also to the professionals who gave their time to check that the book's information was aligned with their areas of special expertise: Noel Adams, Douglas Beattie, Joan Brennan, Doris Brett, Dr Neville King, Helen McGrath, Pauline McKinnon, Dr Harry Marget, Professor Peter Phelan, Professor Margot Prior, Jenny Rickard, Ruth Roselian, Dr Michael Weisenburger, Dr Suzanne Weisenburger and Dr Eleanor Wertheimer.

Thanks, too, to all my colleague fear busters: Robyn Glover, Michelle Moore, David Smith and Pam Tipping; and to all the visitors to our clinic who have put our 'good ideas for busting fears' into practice.

We would also like to acknowledge the inspiration from the Excellerated Learning Institute.

Attention helping professionals

There are existing textbook overviews of children's fears but these are usually very technical. This new book offers a 'cook-book' approach which professionals can apply indirectly to their clients (by devising a plan for use in treatment) or directly (by asking clients to read the book and make their own plan).

Contents

How to use this book

All parents want their children to be confident and happy and it is very distressing not to know how best to comfort a scared child. This book helps you to understand and help overcome your child's fears with practical, step-by-step strategies which have not previously been available in a user-friendly form.

The twelve 'Good Ideas for Busting Fears', which are applied to the very common childhood fears of the dark, of being abducted and of dogs, can be adapted to work with any problem. Parents are invited to first read the whole book carefully. Next read the special children's section *with* your young child or encourage older children to read it for themselves. Discuss the real-life case studies in story form and the cartoons and play the suggested games with your child.

At the end of the children's section the reader is encouraged to design his own 'plan to be fear-proof'. This could be photocopied and pinned up on a bedroom wall to be used as a prescription for coping with fear. The 'Fear-Buster Supreme Certificate' is provided as a reward for successfully overcoming a fear.

Caution: Fear is a very sensitive issue, especially with children. Attempts to prevent fears can sometimes misfire and actually make the fear worse. So it is important that you read the material before going through it with your child, and that children do not study it immediately before going to bed.

PART ONE

for

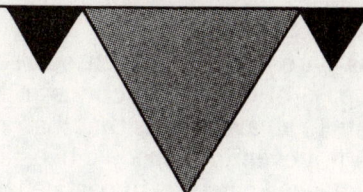

PARENTS

Introduction

Can you understand and help overcome your child's fears? At a Melbourne workshop on this topic a concerned mother said:

> My child has become very frightened since the abductions, especially since the latest one which was in our area. She doesn't sleep through the night, and comes crying and gets into our bed during the night. We tried leaving the lights on — it was no help. She really is fearful that 'Mr Cruel' will come and get her and we won't hear her screams.

How did this parent feel? She felt scared and helpless. At that time a spate of child abductions in Melbourne had alerted all parents to an awareness that their children simply were not safe — not even in their own beds at night.

Times have changed since, as in past generations, parents could reassure their children:

> Never fear, nothing can get you. You are safe, Mum and Dad will protect you.

In those days children's fears really were only in their minds: fears about the dark, ghosts and 'bogeymen'. Nowadays, the fear that an intruder could steal your children out of their own beds is justified and child abductions are on the increase. We have had a stream of clients at our Melbourne psychology clinic who are concerned about their extremely distressed children who are not willing to sleep alone in their own rooms.

How do you feel? It is no longer safe to send children down to the corner shop for the bread or milk. Responsible parents take care that they know at all times where their children are and who they are with. All Australian children are taught about 'Stranger Danger' at primary school. Television shows graphic depictions of the real-life victims of crime daily.

Parents are not only becoming concerned about their children's fear, they are beginning to feel angry and helpless in the face of questions like these:

▲ How do you explain to your children that the next world war will not destroy them? Does it make any difference if it is going on on the other side of the globe? Children know that, with nuclear warfare, there would be no hope.

▲ How can you monitor your children's TV watching so that they don't happen to see extreme and real-life war incidents?

▲ How can you safely go for a jog at six o'clock in the morning if there is no other adult in the house?

As well as these dilemmas, parents also have to deal with the ironic fact that they may not be safe themselves.

How can you help with your children's fears when you don't have the answers yourself? I wish I knew the answers and could give them to you in this book. Instead, I will try to present the basic understandings that psychologists have learned about how fear is caused, expressed and can be treated.

The fundamental philosophy which underlies the message of this book is that the best teachers of children are their own parents and that the best protection against fearful events is education, understanding and communication.

It is a challenge for parents to walk the fine line between allowing children to take risks and protecting them from harm, but children need to learn to protect themselves. Learning comes from taking risks and succeeding, and from making mistakes and correcting them next time.

Children who have confidence in their ability to master and control events and challenges in their lives are less vulnerable to fear.

Janet Hall

5

2

What is fear?

The fight or flight response

Fear and anxiety are absolutely normal and natural emotions. The release of the hormone adrenalin signals the 'fight or flight' response, depending on how the brain interprets the situation; for example:

▲ A small child might see an oversized puppy as a scary moving object. For that child it is time to flee — to run to mother.

▲ To a young boy, the same outsized puppy might be a signal for an exciting game of racing and chasing. For him it is time to fight — to have a fun wrestle.

In these cases it is the same hormone which produces the different feelings, thoughts and behaviours.

A certain amount of anxiety or fear is useful when it enables us to do our best. In public speaking, for example, the butterflies in your stomach can often signal either an excited, enthusiastic feeling or absolute dread.

▲ For people who are confident and well prepared, it is a signal that it's about to be 'show time'.

▲ For someone who is terrified, inadequately prepared or has been laughed at in a similar situation in the past, the same butterflies can be a signal for complete collapse and hysterical refusal to participate.

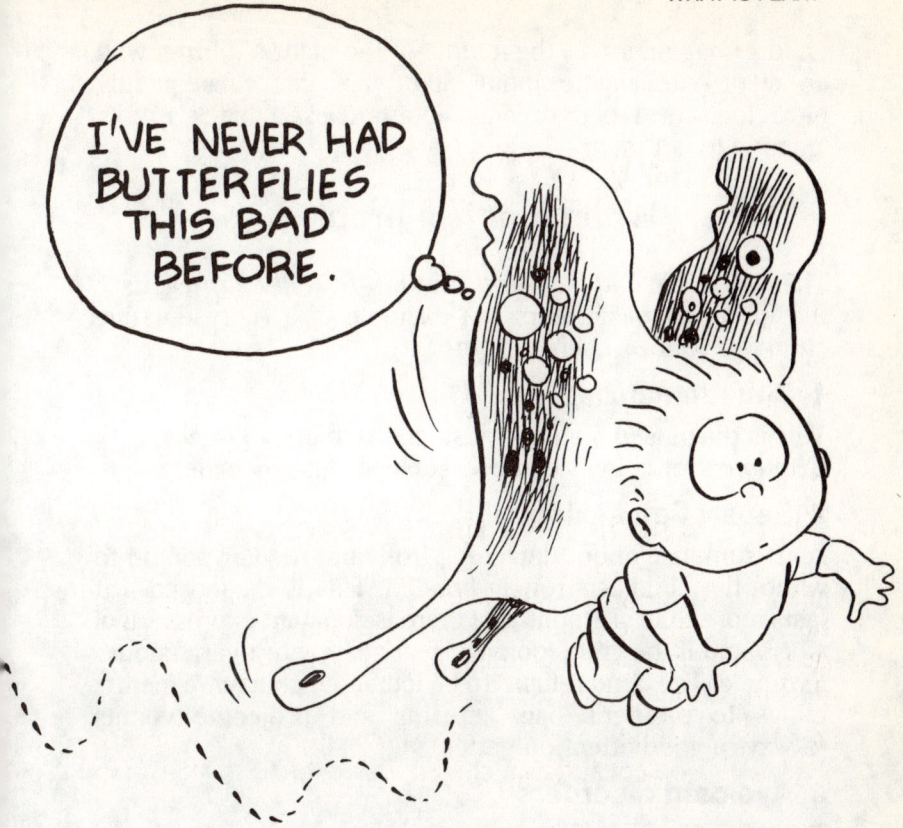

I'VE NEVER HAD BUTTERFLIES THIS BAD BEFORE.

Handy hint: It's not a problem having the butterflies, as long as you can get them to fly in formation!

People seek out fear

Why do vampire movies and Stephen King horror novels do so well? People are excited and gain great emotional release by having their fear levels raised by that kind of stimulation, as long as it's in a controlled context and 'it' can't really get them!

This phenomenon can backfire for our children. A movie that is exciting when viewed during the daytime on a video or in a cinema can be frightening when it is replayed in the

7

child's imagination in the middle of the night. Children who are very enthusiastic about 'Star Wars' can subsequently have long-term bad dreams about masked black robots 'coming to get them'.

When fear is a problem

The *Diagnostic and Statistical Manual (DSM-III-R)* categorises the following basic fears (an example of a representative child fear follows each category).

1 Situation anxiety

This is diagnosed if anxiety lasts more than two weeks.
Example: Not going to flute lessons because of anxiety.

2 Separation anxiety

Fear is intense about detaching from a particular person to whom the child is strongly bonded. This is diagnosed if it lasts more than six months, if there is constant expression of worry and if the child looks tense, unhappy or overanxious.
Example: The child refuses to be left at the child care centre, clings to mother's bag, screams and projectile vomits (always a good attention-getter).

3 Avoidant disorders

These are identified if the anxiety lasts more than six months and there is intense fear about mixing with peers and relating to them socially.
Example: The child refuses adamantly to go to school sport and will undergo *any* 'preferable' punishment instead.

4 Phobias

It is very important to distinguish between an anxiety disorder and a full-blown phobia. Fear becomes a phobia when the fear is totally out of proportion to the reality, there is no voluntary control, there is no obvious reason why the fear started, the person avoids some thing, person or behaviour, and, most importantly, when it interferes with normal living.
Example: A child would have arachnophobia if her fear of spiders was so strong that she could not stay in the same room as a spider or even watch one on television. (Admit it — some parents are 'spiderphobic' too!)

Fear symptoms in children

Three basic sets of symptoms may be clearly evident in a fearful child.

Physical symptoms

- sleep disturbances
- bowel disturbances
- eating disturbances
- tiredness
- breathing upsets like asthma
- headaches and migraines

Emotional symptoms

- fear
- sensitivity
- low self-esteem
- helplessness
- confusion
- despair
- anger
- sadness
- guilt

Behavioural symptoms

- sleep disturbances
- withdrawal
- poor school or academic performance
- aggression
- easily startled
- avoiding going out
- dependence on being close to something
- staying in parents' bed

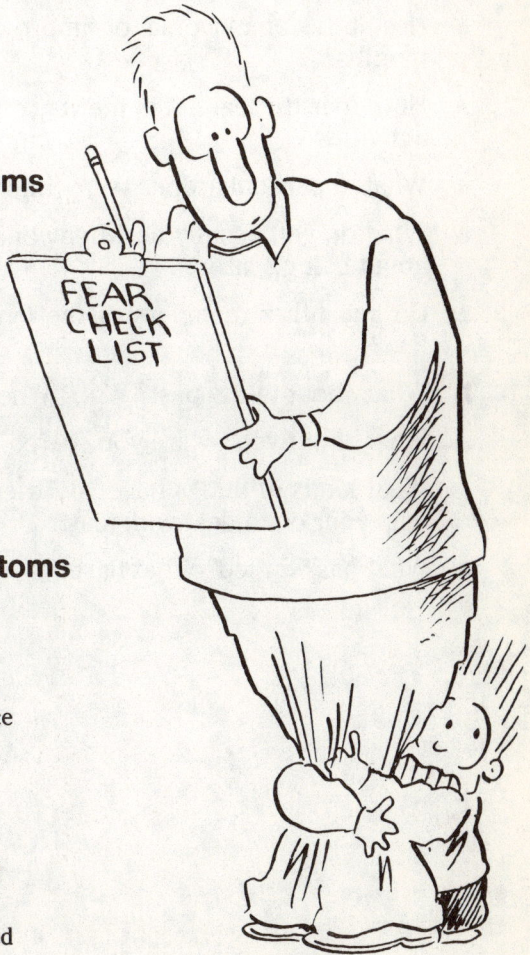

Identifying your child's fears —
Parent's checklist

Describe your child's specific fears:

▲ What behavioural, physical and emotional fears are there (see symptoms list)?

▲ How long has your child felt this way?

▲ What do you think first caused this fear?

▲ Has it become worse or improved in the last three months?

▲ How does the fear get in the way of your child's everyday activities?

▲ What in particular does your child complain about?

▲ What do you usually do when your child is complaining about being scared?

▲ Do any other members of the family currently exhibit fear?

▲ What about in the past? Who? When?

▲ What about you — are you scared?

▲ What kinds of things have you tried to do in the past to help your child deal with fear?

▲ What has worked? What hasn't?

3

The causes of children's fears

Developmental causes

The following table sets out the types of fears most common at certain developmental ages for children.

Developmental age	Type of fear
Infancy	• strangers
	• separation
	• loud noises
	• bright lights
Pre-school and school age	• animals
	• insects
	• the dark
	• doctor/dentist
	• heights
	• monsters
	• nightmares
	• schools
	• storms
Adolescence	• physical injury
	• social relationship
	• inferiority
	• school

SHE'S VERY ADVANCED. SHE'S ALREADY SCARED OF MONSTERS.

According to their stage of development, children will understand things differently. Reassurance does not help until the child has an accurate idea of the event or its causes. We need to correct any misunderstandings.

▶ Case study

A 10-year-old girl refused to go into her bedroom at night. She was sure that a burglar was going to get her in the middle of the night.

The fear started when her friend came to school and told how her own family had come home after an expedition, to find that their house had been ransacked. The school friend described in lurid detail every bit of mess that the burglar had left; every space violation he had made. The young girl was terrified in case somebody got into their house and messed her things up like that.

Suddenly it was discovered that the school friend had *made up the whole story*. Indeed, there had been no burglar; no ransacking!

Unfortunately the young girl was still left with the terrifying fear. (See Rebecca's story on page 76).

Modelling

Children, like adults, learn from what they see other people do. We don't have to actually have experiences ourselves. Modelling comes from things that we read, things that we watch on television and movies and things that we see others do and hear others say.

▶ **Case studies**

Suzie, aged 5, had a phobia about spiders. She would run screaming from any tiny creature with spidery features. Suzie's mother was also scared of spiders and would pick her up and run hysterically from the house, refusing to go back inside until the spider had been removed.

Marie, aged 11, was always complaining about a sore tummy and headaches, and was scared to try anything new. Marie's mother was scared of every single thing, it seemed, but most of all that something bad would happen to Marie. The mother had been deserted by her husband when Marie was only 6 months old. Mother had then poured all her love and attention onto Marie. At the age of 11 Marie had never slept overnight at a friend's house. Her mother picked her up every day straight after school. The mother needed psychological treatment to enable her to cope day by day with her fears that something bad would happen to Marie whilst she was at a camp!

The reward of attention

The psychological principle of reward says that if a consequence increases the likelihood that a behaviour will occur again, then that consequence must be a reward. If a child cries at night, for example, and the mother comes into the room and spends some time being loving and asking the child all about her concerns, the mother is rewarding the crying behaviour. Crying may recur the next night in the hope that the same attention will be received.

I know that this is very hard for some parents to face. You believe that you are doing the best thing to go to a crying child, and certainly if the child has genuine fear, he deserves to have some support and affection … but it is a Catch 22 situation! How does a parent know when it is a case of genuine fear or when the child is playing on the drama?

Because it is very difficult to be really sure, it is probably best to offer the child some verbal reassurance and arrange all the 'security-blanket' props needed for the child to go to sleep. Spend as short a time as possible doing this and arrange to talk about it again the next morning.

Phobias may be maintained because there is a reward value included in avoiding the phobic situation, as in the following case.

▶ **Case study**

Five-year-old Sally had not had any particular trauma. It wasn't certain where she had learned her fear. The one certain thing was that Sally's reaction was excessive. The family couldn't go for a walk or visit neighbours and they couldn't even go to the beach in summer, because the beach was crowded with dogs.

Whenever she saw a dog, Sally crossed to the other side of the road or demanded that her mother pick her up. She was getting a bit too heavy to be carried and her mother insisted that Sally keep walking.

She was unprepared for the extreme reaction that she got. Sally threw herself on the ground, kicked and screamed, had a huge tantrum, and then virtually jumped up onto her mother, screaming and clinging to her neck.

With all of this embarrassment, mother said, 'O.K., O.K., Sally, we won't have to go past the dog,' … and went home again.

Sally avoided the dog by carrying on a treat. By giving in and taking Sally home again, Mother rewarded Sally's extreme tantrum and fear behaviours. Unfortunately, the next time Sally sees a dog, it's likely that she will tantrum even more.

Trauma

Parents want to protect their children from extreme upsets. Life is sometimes cruel, however, and children can be caught up in emotionally and physically traumatic episodes, like car crashes, cyclones, hospitalisations and dog attacks.

Natural disasters

Children who were involved in the Newcastle earthquakes evidenced an increase in bedwetting. Counsellors had to be called in to talk to these children about their fears.

Dog attack

▶ **Case study**

Mark, aged 8, was helping his sister feed scraps to the nextdoor neighbour's dog when the dog suddenly turned on Mark and savagely mauled him.

Mark had to have six plastic surgery operations on his body and was left with massive scarring. As a result, the other children laughed at him when he wore a swimming costume. It was no wonder that Mark was extremely scared of dogs.

Hospitalisation

▶ **Case study**

Tom, aged 3, had a long period of hospitalisation. At first he protested with extreme screaming and crying when his mother left him there. She wanted to stay but had to work and there was nobody else to care for her other children.

For some time Tom would just sit and watch with his eyes full of pain and hurt as his mother left, and finally there was detachment (an observer would hardly even see any reaction) as his mother left.

The bond between mother and child was broken. Tom didn't seem to care whether he saw his mother or not. When he was discharged from hospital however, he developed an acute fear of loss of his father. Whenever his father had to go away on trips, Tom would cause a huge scene, holding onto his father's leg as he left the house.

Imagination

A child's imagination is a source both of joy and fear. Imagination can create a wonderful world of fantasy, a place where anything is possible and you can have anything you want.

Unfortunately this place is also often inhabited by darkness, and in the dark move scary creatures who are out to get you — goblins, elves and the like. Even though a child learns that these creatures in story books really don't exist, when the light goes out and the dark draws around, the imagination runs riot. Anything seems possible and the child is certain that 'those' creatures are about to crawl onto the bed at any moment.

Regression

Some children will regress into younger behaviour when something upsetting happens to them. As a result of their fear or upset, a behaviour emerges which is not age-appropriate.

▶ **Case study**

Sam, aged 9, had been toilet trained at the age of two and a half and was doing extremely well in his family life and at school, when suddenly his duck died.

Sam started to stutter and wet the bed. He also started to express fears about his own death.

The archetype

What do you do if you see a snake slithering across the floor to you? Do you stop to think?

Instinctively we react with fear to some things. Human beings are programmed to react in this way in order to maintain survival. So it's *appropriate* that children are scared of anything that looks reptilian, like snakes and crocodiles and maybe even frogs. It's also appropriate to be scared of heights.

Indeed, some parents are not necessarily comfortable about children who are *not* scared of heights. It's very helpful to parents when children have a respect for heights.

A FOOLPROOF
Menu
TO MAKE A CHILD FEARFUL AND ANXIOUS

Entree

Be born a sensitive child and come from a highly strung family of nervous people.

Have over-protective parents who feel guilty and try to make it up to you by smothering you.

Main course

Have parents who reward you with attention for your fearful behaviours. For instance:

> When you go to bed you can always get your parents to stay in the bedroom with you until you go to sleep.

> If you cry at night and complain about fear of 'something that is going to get you', your parents allow you to crawl into their bed at night.

Have bad feelings of foreboding during the day.

Have low self-esteem.

Have friends at school who, at recess times, talk about all the scary things that might happen to you.

Dessert

Watch a TV show about a horror story.

Have no firm bedtime or routine.

Have nightmares at night.

How parents perpetuate children's fears

Force

A father threw his 7-year-old son in the deep end of the pool. *'You'll have to learn to swim if you're in the deep water'*, said the father as justification.

Ridicule

Father screamed at the kid standing on the diving board, *'Don't be a wimp! Jump in!'*

Punishment

Mother said, *'If you don't eat your dinner up, I'm going to put you outside where the goblins can get you.'*

Ignoring

Daughter was too scared to go to the toilet by herself. Mother ignored her pleas to be helped, 5-year-old wet her pants and it dripped all over the floor.

Overprotection

A mother never let her 11-year-old child stay overnight, ever. *And* took her to school and picked her up. *And* would not let her go on school camp.

4

Strategies for helping your child overcome fear

Parents can do much to help their children cope with fears. Some things are preventive (such as being a good listener and model) and some are curative (such as teaching self-talk and relaxation). The parent's checklist, 'Good ideas for busting fears', suggests twelve ways to help your child. A child's checklist is also provided on page 108 — read it to see the parallels between the two lists.

Good ideas for busting fears: Parent's checklist

What parents can do to help scared kids

1 Listen

Be available and open. It is best to have 'big talks' in the daytime.

2 Protect and comfort

Make sure your child's environment is safe and secure.

3 Teach the facts

Teach your child to have a healthy respect for animals and insects and to tell the truth about strangers.

4 Have a routine

Children thrive on rules and structure — then they know what to expect.

5 Rewards

Children will make more effort and be more willing to take risks if they are motivated by rewards.

6 Modelling

Demonstrate your confidence in the safety of your world.

7 Self-talk

Teach the child to talk through fears, which is a good way of coping.

8 Relaxation

Teach your child to relax and release the tension which fear produces.

9 Stories

Children's stories are full of heroes who cope with or overcome fear — read them together and talk about them.

10 Harness the imagination

Children can defeat anything scary in their imagination.

11 Exercise

As well as being physically healthy and enjoyable, exercise is the universal antidote for high anxiety.

12 Use drawings

Children can both express and 'boss' their fears in drawings.

1 Listen

The best time to listen to children's fears is during the day time. 'Deep and meaningfuls' (heart-to-heart talks) late at night can be intensely upsetting and parents can be led into all sorts of drama and pathos because of the low biorhythms which naturally occur in the night and children's need for attention at bedtime. ·

Parents have to find a balance between being there to listen to a frightened child and being manipulated by a schemer who wants to stay up late! Never ignore a scared child at night, but set a time limit for talking about upsetting things and don't get caught up in night-time drama.

Make a time during the day to sit down with your child and talk about things that might be scaring her. Acknowledge your own feelings about things that have been worrying you or things that you're scared about.

Please note: I am not telling you not to talk to your child. I am just saying to choose the right time so that the best result will be gained for everybody. If you try to have a deep and meaningful conversation late at night, you could be asking for trouble.

2 Protect and comfort your child

Protection and safety

Arrange your household with total safety in mind for everyone:

▲ A child who is scared to stay in bed at night because he might be taken away by a stranger needs to know that the bedroom windows can close.

▲ Teach the child how to use the alarm system.

▲ Make sure that there's a security door.

▲ Keep dangerous objects, especially knives and guns, hidden so other children can't be threatened with them.

▲ Always know where your children are and who they are with.

Comfort

The most reassuring comfort comes from being held by somebody who loves you, being held, touched or rocked.

A calm, loving voice speaking in a hushed, loving tone, telling you that you're safe, works miracles in soothing a frightened body.

The miracle cure

Remember the magical power of the Band-aid? If Band-aids can do miracles with cuts, imagine what they can do with fears! Just sticking a Band-aid on can reassure a young child, because they know that they are being cared for and watched over. They can just touch the Band-aid to feel good about their mother and father being close.

Warning! Ask the child *where* they would like to have the Band-aid (preferably not on a hairy bit that will hurt when it comes off).

The magic of comforters

Some adults are embarrassed when their own parents remind them that when they were babies they had a special comforting object — a teddy, doll or even a piece of blanket or blanket ribbon.

The power of comforter objects is absolutely awesome. To a small child the comforter is the magic fix-all. It helps you go to sleep, to go outside to play, to curl up on mummy's lap and to feel safe and, of course, it knows all your toys and everything that you're doing.

While comforters can be as good as a magic wand when they're there, if they're lost, all chaos breaks out.

Parents need to treat comforters as if they were a major strategic weapon needed for a military advance plan. You

need your back-up reserves! If the comforter is a blanket, for example, and you need to wash it, you might need to tumble it dry to make sure it's available by night time.

Handy hint: To wean children off a blanket, progressively cut it down until, in the end, they only have a tiny piece that you can pin onto their bedclothes at night.

If your child's comforter is a dummy, have several on hand when you go out. Most children grow out of dummies by the age of four. After that it's considered socially inappropriate. Imagine the field day kids would have laughing at your child if she went to primary school with a dummy still in her mouth!

Note: Duplicate copies of comforters are highly recommended but are not easy to get in practice. How is a parent to predict what a child is going to become obsessed with as a comforter? What if the fixation is with the blanket that you bought on the trip to Mexico? Where do you get another one of those?

---

3 Teach the facts

About war

When some young children in Australia became very scared about the Gulf War in 1991, it was found that they didn't know that the Gulf was on the other side of the globe. They thought that it was in the next state and that advancing soldiers would descend upon them at any time. To reassure them, it was recommended that their parents sit down with an atlas (or a globe of the world) and show the child how far away the Gulf is. (Of course, with nuclear war, we know the distance doesn't make any difference.)

About death

Children need to learn about death. If it's appropriate, a child can be allowed to see the dead body. Many hospitals now allow children to go and visit the body if a baby dies.

Children love to conduct their own funerals for animals or creatures which die at home. There's a delightful story about some children who were crying about their dead turtle until their father encouraged them to have a funeral. They turned the whole thing into a festive occasion with a marching band, biscuits and lemonade and had a great time.

Stranger danger

Children certainly need to learn about stranger danger and it's very commendable that there are programmes about it in schools now.

Children also need to learn that it's often not a stranger who can interfere with or hurt them, but a relation or family friend. Although it's very hard for parents to talk about this possibility, children still need to be told the truth.

4 Have a routine

Routines and rituals can be really very reassuring and give a sense of security and safety.

Young children can become very dependent on dummies and security blankets. While this can be extremely frustrating for a family when the loved object gets left behind, children deserve to have their special symbol of reassurance close to them at all times.

If desperate, you can always tell your troubles to the 'Worry Dolls'. In Guatemala the natives make tiny dolls as big as your fingernail which live in a little wooden patterned box. Before you go to bed each night, you tell each doll one of your worries and pop it in the box. When the dolls are in the box you put the lid on and go to sleep. During the night the dolls take care of your problems, so the next day when you wake up you can be happy and relaxed, knowing that your problems are being dealt with.

You can buy Guatemalan dolls in many retail stores, *or* you could make your own — maybe with your child. What a good reason to share some fun, quality time!

Probably you'll enjoy telling the dolls *your* worries too, so you can get a good night's sleep.

The following game is a lovely ritual to establish before going to sleep.

THE
'Good night, sleep tight'
GAME

Parent and child take turns to say three things:

1 One nice thing about today.

2 One nice thing about tomorrow.

3 One nice thing about yourself.

And then you say, 'I LOVE YOU'.

5 Rewards

Rewards can work to overcome fear if the value of the reward outweighs the strength of the fear or the amount of attention the fear receives.

For example, a child can be encouraged to let go of the side of the pool and grab hold of the kickboard if the parent says, 'If you let go, I'll let you watch your favourite show and stay up late tonight'.

It's amazing what the promise of a jellybean can do, too! It all depends on what is rewarding for that child. Some children relate very well to praise — some children need more substantial reinforcements for them to take a risk.

Well done!
You're terrific!

6 Modelling

Modelling, or learning from watching others, is a very strong method of learning. It can be approached through three media.

1 Still pictures

Any photograph or drawing can represent the feared object, including stylised drawings, photographs and cartoons.

2 Moving pictures

These can include movies and TV.

3 Real-life events and situations

You can arrange confrontation of fearful events in real life, *as long as safety is considered*. After all, you'd be crazy to get out of your car in the middle of a lion park!

There are two kinds of models that we can learn from: the 'master model' and the 'coping model'.

The master model

The master model has mastered all the skills, has no fear at all, and is found in movies like 'Superman' and 'Star Wars'. These characters have no fear and can do anything or create any effect that they want.

Examples in real life of people who have mastered skills may include dog handlers, athletes and teachers.

▶ Case study: Using modelling to reverse a phobia

The 8-year-old, Mark, who had been badly mauled by a dog, attended our clinic for treatment. We have a dog in our family (we call it a Clayton's dog: the dog you are having when you are not having a dog), a chihuahua called Jellybean. Now Jellybean is so small that to an adult, and even to an 8 year old who doesn't have a phobia and hasn't been through the terrible trauma of being mauled by a dog, she would be no threat whatsoever. To the 8-year-old-boy, however, Jellybean was a source of great fear.

The master model

Pamela, aged 10, was chosen as the 'master model' to help with Mark. Pamela is so much in love with Jellybean that she often carries her around inside her jumper. By her confident handling of Jellybean, Pamela demonstrated to Mark that there was absolutely nothing that he needed to fear.

After several visits, Mark was able to allow Pamela to hold Jellybean in front of him and was even able to hold Jellybean himself. He was not happy to be alone with Jellybean, though, or to have her running around his feet.

Coping model

A 'coping model' is somebody who is not exactly happy about having to confront a fear, but is determined to get through it somehow and uses coping self-talk.

Coping self-talk moves through four stages

1 Fear alert: what exactly is scary?

2 Counterdefence: what is true and rational?

3 Positives: what is positive and easy?

4 Self-reward: congratulate yourself for coping.

▶ **Case study**

Robin, aged 8, was the ideal demonstrator of a coping model for Mark, who was still scared of Jellybean. Robin was coached in how to interact with Jellybean. It went something like this:

Fear Alert: 'Oh, I don't like Jellybean running around. Look at how big her teeth are. I wonder how sharp they are. They are very pointy.'

Counterdefence: 'Oh well, she is really only a little dog. Nobody else is scared of her. I know that if I keep still she won't jump up on me, and I can take big steps and get away from her really easily and just shut the door on her.'

Look for the positives: 'She is really quite cute. Look at those bulby eyes and that little soft nose, and she is quivering. I wonder if she wants to be patted.'

Self-reward: 'Ah, gee, I really am doing very well. My mum and dad would be proud of me. I wonder what would happen if I picked Jellybean up.'

At this stage Robin picked the dog up and even allowed her to lick his cheek.

After several sessions of watching Robin demonstrate this coping model, Mark was able to pick Jellybean up. Although he had conquered his fear of small dogs, he was still fairly fearful of big dogs. We felt that this kind of fear was probably appropriate, however, because there *is* a genuine concern about approaching a big dog loose in public.

(Read 'Peter's Story' on page 96 for another example of the coping model.)

Warning: Big dogs *can* be dangerous sometimes. There are times when children need a healthy respect for them.

Parental confidence is catching

Children's minds are a blend of reality and fantasy, with fantasy often winning out. When fantasies result in terrors that become chaotic, children feel out of control. It is this feeling of helplessness that is the worst part of being scared — worse than the actual fear itself.

Show your child your own sense of inner strength and confidence. Take control of yourself and your environment. Remember, above all, that you are your child's best model!

The key to helping children deal with fear is to give them a model who portrays a sense of control.

Summary

Psychologists have found that the best results in managing fears occur when the fear is confronted in a real-life situation, but with a phobia it is almost impossible to ever get to that stage. Frightened people need to work their way up to it slowly and gradually, perhaps by first confronting the feared thing in a still picture, then in a moving picture, then in reality.

7 Self-talk

The power of self-talk

Society sometimes laughs at people who talk to themselves, but self-talk is a very appropriate skill for coping with fear or anxiety. It is reassuring to talk yourself through each step as you confront something that frightens you.

Warning: Because people might otherwise think you are a bit strange, use self-talk very softly or under your breath!

▶ **Case study**

A child who has to present a talk in front of a class could use self-talk in this way:

I'm going to be good today when I do my talk. It is only to my teacher, who I know very well, and all my class friends really do want me to do well. I really enjoyed all their talks. It is going to be very easy and I am going to enjoy it.

Affirmations

The power of affirmations or positive thoughts has been strongly recommended in self-motivational and psychological literature. Indeed, people in sales and management have been using affirmations to create positive events in their lives for many years.

You can teach your child to develop her own affirmations. Here are some suggestions.

AFFIRMATIONS
for
KIDS

Next rainy afternoon, spend some time with your child making affirmation cards.

▲ Cut out rectangles of paper and write out, beautifully and colourfully, some positive thoughts.

▲ Affirmations are always written in the positive and as if they are already occurring.

▲ Some examples of positive affirmations for scared kids would include:

I can sleep comfortably and happily all night.

It's easy to sleep easy.

My room is safe.

My world is safe.

I am always protected.

I am powerful and capable.

I have a magic mind.

Self-talk and the darkness test

The 'darkness test' was designed to assess how long children could stand being in the dark alone. The parent puts the child through the test in the child's own bedroom about two hours before bedtime, saying something like this:

> 'Go into your bedroom and sit or lie down on the bed. I'm going to turn the light out and you have to stay in the room as long as you can. If you get too scared, don't try to turn on the light; just come out. You can come out any time but try and be as brave as you can. I'll be just outside. Don't call out. If you are scared, just open the door and come out.'

The test lasts for 180 seconds at the most. After the darkness test, children can rate how afraid they feel on the 'fear thermometer' opposite.

Teach your child to use self-talk during subsequent darkness tests; for example:

Fear alert: 'It's scary in the dark. I want my Mum.'
Counterdefence: 'Oh well, I'm OK. Mum's very close by. I am safe.'
Look for positives: 'This is a good time to relax my eyes. I'll just close them.'
Self-reward: 'Golly, I really am doing well. Mum will be proud of me. I'll just wait for her.'

Naming the problem

You can help your child to get a sense of control over something scary by giving it an absurd name. It's difficult to be scared of something that sounds funny. For example, if your child is scared of some stairs at your neighbour's house, call them something like 'the tricky squiggly stairs'. Or, if your child is scared of the deep end at the public swimming pool, call that 'the silly big kids' end'. Only silly big kids swim there, jumping on each other and hurting themselves — kind little kids swim in the shallow end. So a mother can say, 'Don't go near the silly big kids' end'.

Three more techniques for children to use to feel safe in the dark are the Touching Game, the Naming Game and the 'Who Am I, Where Am I' Game. On pages 36–8 are instructions for playing these games which you can give to your child.

THE FEAR THERMOMETER

How scared are you most of the time?

Colour in to where you think you are

VERY SCARED

A LITTLE BIT SCARED

10
8
6
4
2
0

MY FEAR THERMOMETER

THE
Touching
GAME

The Touching Game is played just before you go to bed. You go around your bedroom, touch everything and name it very loudly.

▲ You touch it and you say what it is:
  'This is the bed'. 'This is the cupboard'.
  'This is the window'. 'This is the dressing table'.
  'This is the door'. 'This is my shoe'.

▲ You go around the room naming all the things that are there and touching them.

▲ Then when you are sound asleep, your brain knows exactly where your body is in your bedroom.

THIS IS MY PILLOW

THIS IS MY FEARLESS KID

Just in case you worry that if you did wake up and didn't know where you were — RELAX! — you would very quickly know because your brain could remember where all those things are that you touched.

THE
Naming
GAME

Once you get into bed this is another game play.

▲ What you have to do is look around the room and name all the things you can see, as quickly as you can. Careful, no cheating!

▲ If you have a big gap in time between naming something, then you have to stop and start again.

▲ Most people can name about six things in a row, but see how many you can name.

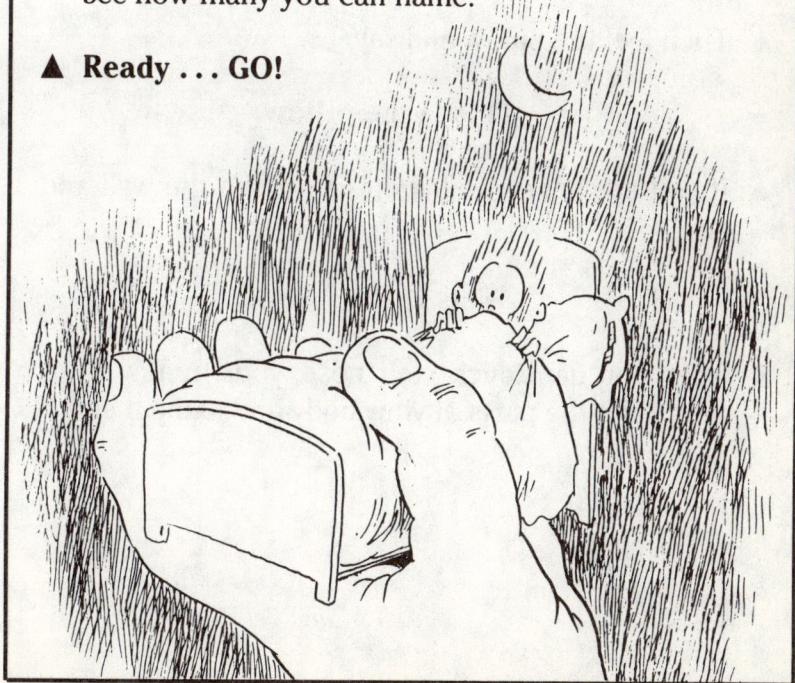

▲ **Ready . . . GO!**

THE
Who Am I?– Where Am I?
GAME

▲ All you need to do for this game is to say:

'My name is ...
(put your name in the blank space)

It's night time and I'm safe in bed.'

▲ Then you can feel the bed and say:

'This is the bed.'

▲ Then feel the pillow and say:

'This is the pillow.'

▲ If you are near a wall, you can touch the wall and say:

'This is the wall.'

▲ Then you can touch your nose, your tummy, your feet ... all the parts of your body and name them.

8 Relaxation

There are two types of relaxation: general relaxation and what psychologists call 'easy/hard list relaxation' or 'systematic desensitisation'. This refers to the technique of having people move through a hierarchy from least to most feared stimulus.

General relaxation

In general relaxation the body, mind and emotions are encouraged to relax in a calm, peaceful atmosphere for consistent periods and over a long time. For example, you could encourage your child to lie down on the bed and read a book for half an hour every afternoon straight after school, as a way of unwinding.

Teaching young children to relax

Most parents have had at least one experience of relaxation, the chance to just lie or sit very well with your eyes closed, breathing deeply.

Relaxation methods often include the progressive relaxing of the muscles of the body. First you relax the hands, then the arms and shoulders, the neck, the jaw, the face and nose, the stomach, and then the legs and feet.

Adults accept this slow progression through the muscles and enjoy the process. You can teach specific relaxation techniques to children but they get bored easily. Children's imaginations need something to work with, so they much prefer to play the 'Floppy Game' or do 'Magic Breathing' — relaxation activities which use the imagination.

THE
Magic Breathing
GAME

▲ First of all you close your eyes … and you just pat your legs and your tummy and your arms and your head …

▲ Then you give your head a little massage, just by rubbing gently behind your ears, and you put your arms slowly, slowly by your side and you start to take big deep breaths.

▲ You breathe with your stomach, so that your stomach moves out and in. Just gently — ever, ever so softly.

▲ As you breathe you imagine that you have holes in your feet.

▲ As you breathe in through your nose or your mouth, the air moves all the way down through your body and then out of the holes in your feet.

▲ Just imagine that the cool air around your nostrils is fresh air and then the air goes in through your nose or mouth all the way down your body, and comes out as warm, lovely … feet breath!!

▲ It's like a nice big circle that goes from your feet, up to your head, through your middle and out again.

▲ You can do 'Magic Breathing' any time, even in the daytime.

▲ If you are waiting for someone or if you are a little bit scared, maybe of a big dog, you can do 'Magic Breathing'.

THE
Floppy
GAME

The Floppy Game goes like this:

▲ Imagine that you are becoming *loose* and *floppy*.

▲ Imagine that your feet can be *flip-flapped* from side to side and that there is a ripple of rubber stuff that moves all the way up through your legs, into your body, through your neck and into your head.

▲ The rubbery stuff makes you feel a bit like jelly. All *loose* and *floppy* and you take a great BIG deep breath and you relax and you feel really good, just like a big bowl of jelly, all loose and floppy.

▲ You're not going anywhere because the jelly is holding you together.

▲ You take another deep BIG breath and you are feeling good; relaxed and comfortable.

Relaxation audiotape

It can be very helpful both for an anxious child and for the parents to regularly listen to a relaxation audiotape. The best tapes are those which have been personalised for the individual with the person's name interspersed throughout the script. Personalised tapes need to be made personally, of course.

How to make your own relaxation tape

You will need two tape recorders. On one, play a piece of beautiful, relaxing music. Speak into the other recorder, making all sorts of suggestions about relaxing and being comfortable, and use your child's name about every minute, as appropriate.

For example, if your child's name is Robin, your story could start like this:

Robin, this is your special time.

This is the time for you to relax and get comfortable and enjoy some lovely music.

Now just imagine that you're breathing in magic fairy dust.

Robin, imagine that Tinkerbell is waving her magic wand and the magic dust spills from the wand and you breathe it in.

So breathe in and count all the way to twenty.

By the time you reach twenty, Robin, you should be feeling very, very relaxed and comfortable.

Relaxation Stories

The following relaxation story can be read to a background of music. It encourages children to relax their muscle parts progressively in a fun way. Encourage your child to join in with the actions. This is based on an idea of Thomas Ollendick*.

RELAXATION STORY

A relaxation story for children goes something like this:

It's a lovely sunny day. A great day to pick lemons.

I reach out my arm and pluck a lemon off the tree. It feels so hard I try to squeeze it. None of the juice comes out, so I squeeze even harder and harder and harder.

Then the juice starts to squeeze out, so I let the

lemon go and then I lick the juice off my fingers. It is yummy.

Just then, I see cat stretching out after waking from his sleep. I decide to have a stretch too. I pull my arms up just like the pussy cat. I have a great big yawn. I push my legs and I push my arms up and then I just fall down on the ground and feel the sun.

It feels so good with my eyes closed, just feeling the sun. It feels like I am a turtle sitting on a rock, nice and warm and safe. All of a sudden I notice a shadow in the sky. I pull my turtle head inside my turtle shell.

There is an eagle flying over. Luckily I see the eagle. I stay inside and just creep my head out very, very slowly. Oh! It is so good. The eagle has gone.

While I am lying here in the sun, listening with my eyes closed, along comes a pesky old fly. I decide I won't pay attention but it sits on my nose.

I wriggle my nose just a little bit. *Shoo fly*. It goes away.

I take a nice deep breath and then that rotten fly comes back again. It comes back this time on my forehead and very gently I start to squeeze my forehead to make it all wrinkly. I think, that will make it hard for the fly to walk. But, whenever I make a wrinkle the fly just jumps off and as soon as I make my forehead smooth again, the fly jumps back on.

Finally, I shoo it right away just in time to open my eyes and see my brother running up.

Oh no, my brother is going to jump on my tummy. I have just enough time to take a breath and make my tummy as hard as I can.

Plop, that doesn't hurt, he gets off again. I take a big deep breath, '*Oooooh, it doesn't hurt really.*'

'*I'll do it again*', says my brother. '*Oww, ooh, ooh*'. This time I hardly have time to tense my muscles up. I tell my brother to go away and he says: '*Aawh, please, can't I play with you. Look here is some bubble gum*'.

Wow, wouldn't you know it, it is my favourite big pink bubble gum, you know the gob stopper type, one that you really have to bite into to get going, it's got that really sweet taste. '*OK*', I say and I pop the gob stopper into my mouth.

I chew and chew and chew. *Oh, it is yum.*

Imagine that you are chewing the bubble gum now.

'*Let's go and play*', I say to my brother.

'*OK*', he says. '*Let's go and play mud puddles*'.

There is a great big mud puddle just near the gate where all the trucks keep coming through. The water is nice as we take off our socks and shoes and roll up our pants legs, the water is nice and warm where the sun has been. The holes are quite deep because there have been many trucks going past. It is a bit like wading in the swimming pool except for the mud that is *oozing* between our toes.

It *squishes* and *squashes* and it feels *verrrrry* good just creeping around our toes and underneath our heels.

Who cares if we get dirty? We think, we can have a bath later on.

It is such fun, we really are having a good time. But then we hear *that* noise. You know. *That* one, 'Children, time for dinner, come in and wash your hands'. It is Mum.

Oh well, I'll come and tell you another story another time. Time for dinner.

The easy/hard list

In this procedure a list is made of about ten items that are frightening to the person being treated. The items are put in order in a hierarchy from least to most frightening.

If professionals administer the hierarchy, they first ensure that the person is relaxed, by playing a relaxation tape or using other relaxation techniques.

Next the professional says, 'Now I'm going to describe a scene. If you are scared, just raise your finger and I'll stop.' Usually the person being treated is so relaxed by the time the frightening thing is described that it doesn't seem frightening any more.

With young children it might be useful to play music, or even offer food and toys, when the scary thing is mentioned and as you work through the list progressively.

On the next page is an example of how Mark progressively confronted his fear of dogs.

THE EASY/HARD LIST: An example

Fear of dogs

Suppose you wanted to help an 8-year-old boy called Mark overcome the fear of dogs which he developed after being mauled by the nextdoor neighbour's dog.

By talking to Mark you would write down a list of scary things that he might do with dogs. Mark could rank them from the least to the most scary. The list might look like this:

1 Suddenly seeing a picture of a dog in a comic.
2 Talking to Mum about going to visit a friend who owns a dog.
3 Seeing a photo of a dog in the paper.
4 Driving past a dog while you're in the car.
5 Seeing a cartoon about a dog on television.
6 Going for a walk in the park and seeing a dog in the distance.
7 Watching a movie about a dog.
8 Being told a scary story about a dog.
9 Watching a person who has a dog on a lead.
10 Patting a dog on the head.

Sleep therapy

A wonderful strategy for parents who have been concerned about their children's night terrors or general daytime anxiety is to use the sleep therapy technique. With sleep therapy the parent goes into the room during the night (perhaps just before the parent goes to sleep) and stands very quietly beside the bed, looking at the sleeping child.

The beauty of the sleeping child never fails to amaze!

What love and joy fills the parent's heart.

Gone completely is the upset of the daytime tantrums and emotional dramas.

There is nothing but love in the space between sleeping child and watching parent.

A really good strategy is for the parent to match his breathing with the child's breathing. This is called 'entering into rapport'.

The parent then says the child's name and just touches the child very gently on the face. The parent then waits and, usually, the child will stir ever so slightly. The parent then says the sleep therapy affirmation.

The sleep therapy affirmation
You are a beautiful, beautiful child, Mary.
(Put in your child's name.)

Mummy and Daddy love you very much.
Sleep easy, sleep well — tomorrow will be a beautiful day.
I love you.

The parent then leaves the room very quietly.

Amazing things can happen the next day as both child and parent carry in their hearts an unconscious memory of the connection that they made in the middle of the night.

9 Stories

Published stories

There are some absolutely wonderful stories in the children's sections of libraries that can be used by thoughtful parents to prevent and manage fears in their children; for example, the picture books *Harry and the Terrible Whatsit* and *Franklin in the Dark*.

Harry and the Terrible Whatsit is about a little boy who is too scared to go down to the cellar. When his mother goes into the cellar to get some pickles, she doesn't come back and Harry is certain that the Whatsit has got her.

Sure enough, when Harry goes down into the cellar, there is a big, huge, ugly, grumpy two-headed Whatsit.

Harry screams, 'Where's my mother?'

The monster looks at him with disdain and says 'What's it to you?'

Harry gets so angry that he starts to hit the Whatsit and pretty soon the Whatsit begins to shrink, becoming smaller and smaller and smaller.

Just as the Whatsit is about to disappear altogether, Harry says, 'Well, why are you disappearing? What's happening here?'

The Whatsit says, 'This always happens. Just when I'm about to do well and scare a kid, they become brave again and pretty soon I start to shrink, and now I'll probably disappear'.

Harry feels sorry for the Whatsit, so he has a think and says, 'Well, look, go next door to Sheldon's house. He's pretty scared.'

So the story ends up with Harry telling his mother (who has gone out a side door into the sunshine to pick flowers) all about how he conquered the Whatsit.

The trick in the end of the story is on the very last page. There is a picture of Harry's house and Sheldon's house and the caption says:

Just then there was a terrible scream from the house next door. Sheldon must have discovered the Whatsit.

Kids really identify with Sheldon's scream and are glad

that the Whatsit has survived to scare another kid another day. Deep down, kids know that a little bit of fear is a motivator!

So, what do children learn from this story? They learn that their imagination can do very amazing things.

In your imagination you can beat up any monster and he will go away!

In *Franklin in the Dark* (which has beautiful soft pictures), Franklin the Turtle spends the day meeting other creatures who are scared.

Franklin is so afraid of the dark that he doesn't even live in his own shell. Instead, he carries it around on the end of a rope.

Franklin meets a duck who is afraid to swim and who has water wings to help, a bird who is afraid to fly and has a parachute to help, a lion who is afraid of noise and who has ear muffs and a bear who is afraid of the cold and wears lots of warm clothes.

When Franklin crawls into his very own shell that night, the reader thinks that Franklin has overcome his fear.

On the very last page, however, there is a surprise twist: 'And just then Franklin turned on his nightlight.'

The story about Franklin describes a coping model. Franklin still needed the help of his little nightlight, just as children might.

Made-up stories

Parents and children can learn a lot about fear and how to prevent and manage it by telling real-life or made-up stories themselves. In our family we used to spend a lot of time travelling and the children would ask us to tell them a story.

We used to choose a problem such as lighting fires, stealing or being taken away by a stranger and base a story on the particular problem. One storyline was about little girls who were clever and silly girls who got into trouble; for example:

The silly girl talked to a stranger in the street and got into his car. She was taken away and badly hurt. The clever girl told the stranger to go to the police station if he wanted directions, and she ran to the nearest safety house.

The silly girl got the matches, lit a fire and burned the house down. The clever girl took the matches from the baby and then told her mother.

Sometimes these stories went on and on, with more and more detail. The moral was always simple and sweet!

Making up your own stories is a lot of fun and children really learn by making up possible outcomes for their own or parents' stories.

Ideas for stories

What stories could you make up? First set the scene, then talk through how children would cope with fear. Give them lots of ideas about practical and imaginary things that they could do; for example:

What would happen if ...

▲ Imagine if you came home one day and found that Mum and Dad weren't in the house?

▲ What if we had been called away unexpectedly, or what if we had got stuck in traffic after there had been a very bad accident and couldn't get through the traffic?

▲ Or what if one of us had broken a leg?

Of course, don't end the story until you have arrived at a positive outcome.

'Annie stories'

Psychologist Doris Brett found that she needed to reassure her daughter about things that were scary. In her book of 'Annie Stories' Doris gives examples for helping children with fears and dealing with traumatic events like nightmares, a new baby, first days at kindergarten, divorce, death, pain and going to hospital.

In these stories, parents make up a story about a situation very like their own child's. The parent tells a story depicting the child's worry or concern and adds a wonderfully successful twist at the end in which the child overcomes her fear.

Picture this scene:

Ten-year-old Sally had to sing in the school concert. She was terrified. Her Mum told her a story, and it went something like this:

Once upon a time there was a little girl called Samantha ... (the name used in the story sounds in essence the same as your child's name) ... who lived in a brick house with a red door knob. Samantha slept in a bed with a pink doona on it. Samantha was scared to go in a school concert because she had to sing a song. Samantha didn't know how she would get over her fear at first, but then she came up with a good plan.

She practised her song, until she knew it. She sang it in the bathroom, she sang it in the toilet, she sang it in bed at night. She practised until she knew it so well that her brain knew that she would never forget the words. Then she went up on the stage every day, and just stood there and practised it in her mind.

She also got herself a 'magic ring' to wear. She asked her Mum if she could wear Mum's special bracelet which Samantha thought was magic.

When it came time for the concert Samantha jumped upon the stage and sang the best of all the children and won the prize. She was so happy and proud of herself.

It is easy for parents to do Annie Stories — you already know the plot, you already know the characters — you are only providing a positive new ending.

A variation on the stories is for the child to tell a sad story, perhaps a true one, and then for the parent to retell the story using the same situation but with a good solution at the end.

Annie Stories allow children to keep a safe distance from their own fear but still let off steam. The story shows them that they're not the only one; that someone else has felt just as bad; someone else understands. It gives them ideas for coping and gives them closeness and comfort with the parent during the story telling.

What about fairytales?

If fairytales seem terrifying, why do children love them? Recent evidence suggests that they can help children with emotional problems.

The psychology behind fairytales is in the way they present pictures to the child's mind. They help children to identify with their own unconscious thoughts, fears, and dreams and the black and white distinctions between good and bad, ugly and beautiful fairytale characters allow a child to see problems as very simple. As a result children can become positive and hopeful, because good usually wins over bad.

Remember that dreams are part of nature's way of helping our minds integrate, project, analyse and experience possibilities. Bad dreams are not necessarily bad experiences — a lot can be learned. All children need dreams, and fairytales help promote them.

Adults need a dream too. (What's yours? Come on ... own up!)

10 Harness the imagination

There are many positive things that you can encourage your child to do with his imagination; for example, he can bash up monsters, as in *Harry and the Terrible Whatsit*, or get rid of the wicked witch by throwing water over her, like Dorothy in the *Wizard of Oz*. Talk about how we can do all those sorts of things to monsters in our imagination. There is a delightful book on this topic called *How to Get Rid of Bad Dreams*, by Nancy Hazbry and Roy Condy. A summary of some of its excellent ideas is given in the list below.

Another book, called *One Night at a Time*, by Susan Hill, is a beautiful picture book about Tom who reads lots of stories.

When Tom reads a scary story about goblins, he has a very bad dream. Tom's mother says, 'They are only pictures in a book. They are not real and they can't hurt you.'

IDEAS FOR YOUR IMAGINATION TO USE:
Brave ideas for scary fears

▲ *If monsters are taking you . . .*

Show the monster its own reflection in a mirror and it will be so scared it will run away.

▲ *If a bad dragon is breathing fiery breath . . .*

Shrink him with your laser gun until he is small enough to take to school as your pet.

▲ *If you dream you are lost in a jungle and sinking in quicksand . . .*

Sip the magic potion that makes you small until you can row your hat out of the quicksand.

▲ *If green and black furry bugs attack you . . .*

Get out a can of silver spray paint, spray them and blow them into the sky to become stars.

▲ *If you are about to fall off a mountain . . .*

Chew bubble gum, stick it to your feet and walk down the mountain.

▲ *If an ugly troll gets you . . .*

Laugh at him and he will be laughing with you and you will become friends.

▲ *If you are trapped inside a giant's nose . . .*

Take a feather from your pet parrot and tickle until the giant sneezes and you can use your umbrella as a parachute.

▲ *As a last resort!*

Jump into bed with mum and dad.

Source: Hazbry N. & Condy R., *How to Get Rid of Bad Dreams*. Text © copyright 1983 Nancy Hazbry. Reprinted by permission of Scholastic Canada Ltd, 123 Newkirk Road, Richmond Hill, Ontario, Canada L4C 3G5.

Tom keeps on having bad dreams. He imagines that the dryer is a monster with things in its tummy and then he dreams about that. Finally his mother tucks him in one night and says, 'I will give you good dreams'. And she does, just by tapping Tom's eyelids.

When Tom goes to stay with his friend Ned, Ned says, 'I have a watch dog so I don't have bad dreams'. (The watch dog was really just Ned's stuffed toy!)

Tom feels so good about Mum's and Ned's ideas that he sleeps happily, even when he is being minded.

When he reads a story about a giant he is a little bit scared that he might have a bad dream about the giant and asks his mother to make sure he won't. She just says, 'One night at a time'.

Dream empowerment

The power of the imagination is amazing. Positive suggestions can certainly be taken up by the mind so that you can actually dream about a prechosen subject. In dream empowerment, you suggest to your child that she will dream positively and will always be the winner in the dream, no matter what kinds of upsets occur in it.

The instant replay

Another good technique, if your child has a bad dream or scary thought, is to ask him to replay the dream or thought in his mind, only this time to make it turn out with the child as the hero, the brave one — the winner. For example:

If there is a monster trying to get the child, he could pull its pants down! Monsters hate to have their bottoms bared in public and an embarrassed monster will always run right away.

With videos freely available in many houses, it is difficult for parents to monitor what children see — adults' videos can sometimes be left in the wrong pack, for example. Once when I was on holidays and my parents were looking after my children they somehow got to watch *The Hunchback of Notre Dame*. When I came home I was amazed to find them talking about a creature called Quasimodo. At first I was not at all pleased that they had seen the film, but I changed my mind when I saw how maturely they handled it. They talked about it a lot, trying to understand why people laughed at the hunchback.

On another occasion they unfortunately got hold of the Jack Nicholson video, *The Witches of Eastwick*. I didn't know that they had been watching it, and when I put them to bed they started to cry and didn't want to sleep apart.

'Why didn't you turn it off if it was scary?' I asked.

Of course, neither they nor I know why they didn't. Why don't I put down a Stephen King book when it's scaring me?

So, to fix the witches we had to start thinking about what we could do with witches. Robin said that he would pull the witch's nose off and Pamela said that she would stick the witch's broom up her nostrils — we fixed that witch 'real good'! By talking about it the children felt in control.

Below are some good ideas for helping your child use her imagination to conquer the witches, goblins, wolves and monsters which often loom large in her fears and dreams.

Getting rid of witches
What if you were scared of witches?
If you were scared of witches you could imagine that a big witch was coming at you just like Dorothy and the Wizard of Oz (did you ever see that movie? If not ask Mum and Dad to let you watch it).

In 'The Wizard of Oz', Dorothy had to kill the witch and she didn't know how. In desperation she threw a bucket of water over her and — wouldn't you know — that was just the one trick that worked ... and the witch melted away.

Getting rid of goblins
What if you had to get rid of a goblin?
Well, goblins don't like to be tickled. You could imagine that when you start to tickle the goblin, he crumples up with laughter. He keeps crumpling and crumpling until in the end, you can flatten him out with your foot and stamp him down just as if he was a bit of paper.

Getting rid of wolves
What if it was a wolf?
Well, wolves don't like fire. So all you'd need to do is light a great big fire and just stay there safely until it is morning. Make sure you've got plenty of wood now.

Getting rid of monsters
What if it was a monster?
You can make any old scary monster thing shrink. All you need to do is just stand up to them and tell them off. Tell them that they're not welcome in your dream. They're not welcome in your space. You tell them to just go away.

Emotive imagery: the superhero story

With emotive imagery, you tell the child a story in which she identifies with a superhero and overcomes all thoughts of terrifying experiences. For example:

▶ **The superhero story**

Superhero wants your help. What does your superhero look like? Nobody else in your family can see your superhero, because he only wants *your* help.

You need to go to sleep first — in your own bedroom — so that you will be fully rested for that special mission. So, imagine that you're in bed and the light is on and you can see the superhero but your Mum can't. Where is he standing?

Warning: If you are scared while I'm telling you this story, all you need to do is lift your little finger.

So, Mum says goodnight and you fall asleep. You wake up in the middle of the night in the dark. It's very quiet and you can only hear your own breathing. You can hear your superhero breathing too, and you know that the Scary Things are there.

Superhero says: 'It's time for the Mission to eliminate all Scary Things.'

You set off together, imagining that you're getting out of bed, and you go over to the window. You see the Scary Things that you have to go and beat outside. You think up all sorts of ways that you're going to beat them and you turn invisible too. In the end, you and your superhero destroy the Scary Things.

You remember that the Scary Things aren't really real — they're only in your imagination. Are you scared of them? No ... you're not, because it's only your imagination and you can do whatever you like in your imagination.

Next thing you wake up in the morning and you've been asleep all night. Your Mum comes in and says: 'I'm so proud of you — you stayed in bed all night.'

And you feel really, really good, and get a reward and a hug.

11 Exercise: the universal antidote for high anxiety

Children should be encouraged to exercise. Anxious children in particular will find that regular exercise reduces their overall anxiety levels.

The benefits of regular exercise include:

▲ improved concentration

▲ increased energy

▲ an attractively toned body, which makes self-image positive

▲ decreased anxiety

▲ decreased hostility

▲ mood elevation

▲ increased immune response and resistance to illness

▲ better sleep

▲ good control of body weight and overall relaxation

Positive spin-offs of exercise for the scared child

Keep your fearful child exercising and tell him that exercise gives him strength, flexibility and cardiorespiratory performance.

This means that if the worst comes to worst, you could run faster than any old monster, bad robber, burglar or big black dog.

---

12 Drawings

Everyone has a natural ability to express feelings through images and many of us can actually draw well. (At least you lucky adults who didn't have a scary teacher criticise your drawings can probably still draw!)

Encourage your child to draw her most scary thought. You may then be able to empathise with just how real *and* how powerfully scary her fears are. Then it's time to help the child to express her own power over the fear. Ideas include:

▲ Burn the scary picture.

▲ Cut it into pieces and scatter them in the wind or over a cliff or flush them down the toilet.

▲ Tip paint or nail polish over it.

▲ Draw it over and over again, but getting smaller each time, until it disappears!

▲ What else? I'm sure that you and your child can have fun bossing fears through drawings and deciding what else you do with and to them.

If you need professional help

How much freedom can you give your child?

Parents have to tread a thin line between granting freedom and setting limits. Kids who are overprotected are prevented from testing themselves out and can't acquire the self-protecting mechanisms necessary for quick thinking if anything goes wrong. Nowadays, however, parents have also to cope with the changes of the suburban rat race. For most of us, as kids, the walk to school by ourselves was a reflection of the trust that our parents had in us. We were independent. Now it's not a matter of trusting your child — you can't trust your fellow humans.

Find your child a 'coach'

Sometimes no matter how competent the parent is, a child refuses to respond to reason; the bond between the parent and child is so strong that the emotions are overwhelming. This is when a child might need a 'coach'. This doesn't have to be a professional, it can be the nextdoor neighbour. Just so long as it's someone who the child relates to, who is willing to listen, give encouragement and motivation and has some time to share.

It's not easy for a parent to resist a crying child who is

too scared to stay in her own room when it's the middle of the night. But the child who knows that a helpful neighbour will ask, 'Well, how did you go last night? Were you able to stay in your own bed?' might be more likely to stay in her own bed.

Questions to ask yourself before seeking professional help

▲ What fears is my child expressing?

▲ How long have the fears gone on?

▲ Has there been any change in the fears?

▲ What was the cause of the fears?

▲ Do the fears affect my child's normal functioning? Do the fears affect my child's success?

▲ What physical symptoms does my child's fear produce?

▲ What behavioural symptoms do my child's fears produce (verbal/non-verbal)?

▲ What do I do in handling my child's fears?

▲ What has worked so far in helping my child with fears?

▲ What has not worked so far in helping my child?

▲ Are there others modelling fear for my child?

Fears can sometimes be useful for parents

Sometimes fears can be very useful, not only to the person who has the fear, but to somebody else in the family. Consider this scenario:

A mother allowed her daughter to sleep with her, in her own bed, for over eight years. The father had abandoned the family when the child was only 6 months old. Until the child was 9 years old, the mother enjoyed having her in her bed, but then she met a man with whom she wanted to live. It is

not surprising that the new man did not want the daughter in the bed with him.

Mother brought the child for psychological counselling. A programme was devised which involved mother following through with standards of behaviour which required steeling her mind against going to the aid of her child, even when the child was calling out or crying.

After four weeks, it was found that the daughter had not moved out of the mother's bed at all. On questioning, the mother said she had not followed instructions and had decided that she didn't like the man any more.

It's interesting to wonder about the mother's real investment in keeping the daughter in bed with her in this case.

Helping your child to recover after trauma

Traumas come in all sorts of ways. Unfortunately in our society some are natural, like bushfires and cyclones, and others are a result of crimes like hit-and-run car accidents, domestic violence and child abductions.

Sometimes children react to such traumas immediately and sometimes behavioural and emotional symptoms appear much later.

Possible symptoms after trauma

▲ fighting amongst brothers and sisters and friends

▲ becoming dependent on family

▲ poor school performance

▲ rigidity — wanting things 'just right'

▲ irritability and aggressiveness

▲ sleep problems and nightmares

▲ reverting to behaviour that the child had outgrown

▲ complaints about being sick

A child might be preoccupied with the trauma. He might want to talk about it all the time, play it out, act it out or want to go back to see where it happened.

What you can do to help

After a trauma, it is very important not to ignore the child's feelings. Allow her to pour out all her emotional upset.

Warning: This is *not* the time for parents to implement behavioural consequences for crying. Those sorts of strategies are highly recommended for long-term behavioural disturbances, but a trauma is a very unusual event and needs to be treated as an exception.

The heartless mother

Picture the following scenario:

Billy, aged 8, runs screaming to the back door, throws down his bag and cries to Mum:
'Mum, Mum — a boy fell over in the school yard today and split his head open!'

Mum looks up and says, 'Put your bag away, Billy'.

Billy runs up to Mum and says, 'You should have seen the blood — I was nearly sick!! The blood went all over the place and the boy was slipping in it and then his eyes closed and he just lay there still. I thought he was dead, Mum!'

Mother: 'Billy, I don't know how many times I've told you to put your bag away. If you don't put your bag away right now, you won't get any TV.'

'But Mum, this has got nothing to do with my school bag. Will you please listen?'

(Mother ignores Billy.)

That night, Billy wakes up screaming, with nightmares. Mother lies in bed and says to father, 'Don't you go to him — I'm fed up with him, he's not doing any of his jobs — he's just crying out for attention!'

There's absolutely no reason for this mother to be so heartless. In the aftermath of a trauma kids need understanding. This is not the time to insist on rules and regulations.

Be a positive parent: programme your child with positives

Be careful not to cause an accident because of your own fear. Many a child has fallen from a tree or fence and broken a limb because a parent has called out, 'Watch out, you'll fall!' Immediately after this call, what happens? Yes, the child falls.

Be careful about your language around children. Always have a positive expectation. The brain does not hear a negative. For instance, it doesn't hear 'don't'. Remember what happens when an anxious mother, watching a three-year-old proudly carrying an overfull cup to the table, says, 'DON'T SPILL IT!'

Yes! You're right, of course. The child spills it.

So, instead of warning with a negative line, such as 'Don't

get hit by a car!', 'Don't drop it and be messy!' or 'Don't get lost', say it positively; for example:

'You will be careful.'

'Take good care'.

'Step carefully'.

'Fear busters' believe in themselves

Help your child to be a 'fear buster' who knows that, in the end, only she can do it — only she can help herself bust through her fear. Fear busters know that:

IF IT IS TO BE

IT'S UP TO ME

One of the most powerful stories for helping children to believe in themselves is *The Magic Locket*. With the book comes a beautiful golden locket for the reader to keep.

The story tells how a little girl is always in trouble. When her aunt gives her a golden locket and tells her to hold it and say, 'I believe in you', everything goes well in the girl's life. One day she drops the locket and it opens to show that inside, there is a mirror! The girl was affirming her own belief in herself.

What a message! Believe in yourself and you can do anything.

Conclusion

Congratulations! You are now an expert in understanding, managing, and preventing fears in children. Now that you know all you need to know, apply that knowledge as best you can. Trust that you will also intuitively know what to say, and when and how to handle fearful situations. Obviously, you are a caring parent. You deserve to acknowledge yourself! Parenting is the hardest job we ever undertake and the one for which we get the least training and no pay!

Thank you for your commitment to helping your child learn to cope with fear. The next section of this book is for children. If your child is not yet reading independently, you can show the cartoons and either read the stories to the child or tell them in your own words. Children aged eight or more will probably prefer to read the three stories and make their own fear-buster plans by themselves.

Remember to keep reading and discussion to daylight hours so your perspective on fears can be maintained. The 'Good ideas for busting fears' list gives strategies which can be adapted to use with any fears, worries, problems or upsets.

Remember, too, that the 'Good ideas for busting fears' list can be just as useful for you! Adapt the strategies in both the parent and child sections of this book to *any* problem, and you can be a 'Fear-buster supreme' along with your child!

PART
TWO
for

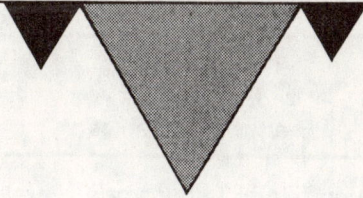

CHILDREN

6

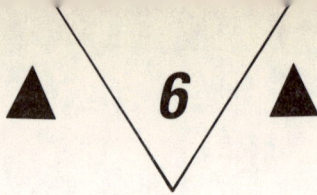

How to be boss of burglars, bogeymen and big black dogs

Introduction

Most kids think that they are the only ones who have a problem. Everyone else seems to be able to be the boss of themselves. They always seem brave and able to boss their feelings and bodies to do whatever they want.

Guess what?
It's all a trick
Everyone gets scared.

How would you like to know some secret ways that you can be the boss of yourself when you get scared?

Here is one way that works: *draw your most scary thing*.

What sorts of things are kids scared of?

It depends how old you are.

Babies
When you were a baby you were scared of loud noises, any sudden thing moving and any bright lights, and you didn't like it much when Mum left you. It was scary to be alone.

Toddlers

When you were about two you thought that *things were going to get you.*

Can you remember sitting on the toilet and thinking that the inside of the toilet was going to bite you on the bottom? Or that you might fall in and disappear and they'd never find you again?

Or was it scarier to think about being flushed down the toilet?

Or scarier to think about being sucked down the plug hole of the bath? Do you remember the first time that slurpy noise happened when the bath water was running out? What about the way that the water pulls at your legs? Did your bottom get sucked over the plug hole and squeeze and hurt and have little red marks?

Kids three years and over

Sometimes little children get very scared of big things, especially if the big things are moving. Often, for example, children of about four get scared that dogs might run up and get them. Even friendly dogs can be scary because they can lick and have smelly breath and jump up on you and scratch you.

It's only natural to be scared of things that might hurt us. The trouble is that sometimes your brain can't really understand the difference between *real* things that hurt us and things that *we make up*.

Sometimes, for instance, we make up an idea that a burglar will get us and take us away. Why are we so scared of burglars when we've never actually seen one?

When we're about three we start to get really good at making up things that scare us. Sometimes we get some ideas from watching TV. We might watch a cartoon or movie about witches or goblins or bad men or burglars.

I CAN'T READ MY FEAR OF THE DARK CHECKLIST. IT'S TOO DARK!

CHILD'S FEAR OF THE DARK
CHECK-LIST

1 How long have you been scared at night?

2 Do you remember the first time you were scared at night?

3 What do you think first caused you to be scared?

4 Have your night time fears been getting better or worse in the last month?

5 What do you do when you get scared at night?

6 What makes the dark scary?

7 What other things are you scared of?

8 When are you most scared?

9 What do your parents usually do when you get scared at night?

10 Does anybody else in your family get scared at night?
Who? When? How? Why? What happens to them?

11 What time do you usually go to bed?

12 Who usually helps you get ready for bed?

13 Are you usually ready for bed when you are told to go to bed?

14 What do you do that can help you feel brave?

15 What does *not* help?

16 What works the best to help you feel brave?

Being scared of the dark

The scariest thing of all is going to bed in the dark. Your imagination is that part of your brain which starts to work when you're in the dark.

What is the dark?

If you put your hands out in the dark can you touch anything? Why aren't we scared of the light? We can't touch it either.

All of the fairy tales talk about the dark as the time when bad things happen.

Hansel and Gretel got lost in the dark. The birds had eaten all their bread and they couldn't find their way home.

Cinderella had to go home at twelve o'clock. That was in the dark. I wonder if she was scared when she ran all the way home? Would you be?

Sometimes fairy tales are very scary. If they're scary, why do we get excited by them? Why do we like fairy tales so much? We even like them when they're *really* freaky and scary, like when the giant was chasing Jack down the beanstalk. Wouldn't that have been scary when the giant hit the ground if you were still on the beanstalk? You might have worried that you might fall off!

Heights *can* be scary. Your fear of heights helps you then, because it reminds you to be careful and hang on!

Sometimes it's healthy to be a little bit scared

Can you imagine walking in the middle of a road with busy traffic? Even if you were really brave and didn't feel scared at all, the cars don't know that. Pretty soon there'd be **squashed you** for breakfast!

What if you went to pat an alligator? It's impossible to tame alligators to be friends, you know. Even if you weren't scared there'd be **chopped-up you** for breakfast.

SO ... Sometimes it's healthy to be very scared of things like being in the middle of the road or patting an alligator.

What other things can you think of that it's healthy to be scared of? Make a list.

Sometimes it's not healthy to be scared

It's not healthy to be scared if you need to do something that everyone else can do and you can't do it because you're too scared.

What if you can't sleep in your bed at night?
Mum and Dad might smack you if you try to get in their bed in the middle of the night. Smacking isn't a very healthy thing is it? So why can't Mum and Dad understand that you're really, really scared? Weren't they ever scared too?

Well, I guess you know that they *were* scared once. They have learned to be boss of their brain.

How can YOU learn to cope and be boss of burglars, bogeymen and big black dogs? AND ... school tests and spiders and heights and ...?
Lots of people are scared about lots of things.

On the next page, in the 'Good ideas for busting fears' list, there are twelve very good ideas for you to start doing so that you won't be scared. You can be brave!

GOOD IDEAS FOR BUSTING FEARS
What you can do if you're scared

1 Talk to somebody.

2 Make sure you have a safe and comfortable space around you.

3 Find out the facts. What's the truth?

4 Know what to expect. How and when to do things.

5 Ask someone to give you rewards when you show that you're brave.

6 Copy people who are brave. People in pictures, photographs, movies and real life.

7 Talk yourself through it.

8 Learn to relax.

9 Imagine facing up to the fear.

10 Read lots of stories that show how people and animals cope with their fear.

11 Exercise.

12 Use drawings first to show and then to boss the fear.

To be brave

Take control of your mind and make your imagination work for you. You can be the boss of your brain and the boss of your body, so be brave and bust through your fears!

You can use these good ideas for anything you are scared of.

△ ⟍7⟋ △
Fear-buster stories

In this book there are three stories about children who were scared once, and used all these good ideas (and even some more) and became brave again. These children were scared about burglars, bogeymen and big black dogs, but it wouldn't matter what you were scared of ... the good ideas can help you to be brave.

The stories you will read are:

▲ Rebecca's Story, which tells how a girl stopped being scared and became boss of burglars.

▲ Sam's Story, which tells how a boy stopped being scared and became boss of bogeymen and things in the dark.

▲ Peter's Story, which tells how a boy stopped being scared and became boss of big black dogs.

When you read these stories *you* will get some really good examples of things to do that will help *you* if *you need* to be *brave*.

Good luck!

REBECCA'S STORY:

Being scared of burglars

How Rebecca got to be scared

Rebecca was terrified to get into her own bed at night. She had watched a TV programme which showed how a burglar had taken a little girl right out of her bed in the middle of the night. When the parents woke up the little girl was gone.

Do you know, they never found the little girl for a long

time? And when they did find her, it was only her body, because she was dead.

Rebecca hated hearing that story. **It was scary.**

At the same time Rebecca heard her friend at school say how one night she'd come home with her family when they'd been out late and they'd found that the whole house had been messed up. **A burglar had been.**

The burglar had thrown all the things out of everybody's drawers, stolen money from the Dad's suit pocket, taken the video, the TV, the stereo and money out of Rebecca's friend's money box, and had even kicked the dog. The dog had a big red hole in its head that was bleeding.

AND the burglar had eaten the strawberry shortcake in the kitchen!

When Rebecca heard about her friend's story, she was sad, mad and scared. She didn't want any burglar coming and doing that to her family.

Rebecca decided that she would have a plan. She would stay awake all night just outside her parents' bedroom door and she would guard the house.

So the first night, when everybody else had gone to bed, she got out of bed and went to guard her parents' door. She was all right walking in the dark until she got to her parents' door because she had a little torch.

But as she stood there hearing her parents breathe, the torch went out. The batteries had gone flat.

She stood there and listened. She could hear all sorts of noises — creaking noises — she thought she heard a noise at the front door. She thought she heard a noise at the window.

She wanted to run back into bed but when she got to the door of her bedroom she thought she could hear somebody trying to get in at her window.

She was so scared she started to cry and ran back into her parents' bedroom. She starting hitting her father and saying, 'I'm scared, I'm scared, let me in, let me in, let me in!'

Her mother and father let her get into bed with them, gave her a kiss and cuddle and said, 'Never mind. It will be all right.'

'But I was only trying to help,' Rebecca said. 'I just wanted to rescue everybody and save everybody from the bad burglar.'

'There's no burglar,' said Dad. 'Come on, I'll take you back to your bed.'

'No, no, no,' she said. 'I don't care if there's no burglar. I'm not going back in my room and that's that.'

By this stage everybody was a bit tired, so Mum and Dad just let Rebecca sleep in their own bed.

The next morning they didn't talk about what had happened the night before and Rebecca felt too embarrassed to tell them what had happened to her.

The next night, the family were out very late and when they got home everybody was tired. Rebecca had been asleep in the car. She felt her daddy taking her up and putting her into her own bed but as she got to the doorway she remembered the burglar trying to get in through the window.

'No, no,' she screamed, and grabbed hold of the door as strong as she could be and wouldn't let her Dad take her in. Her father looked at her mother, who said, 'Just to save the peace let her come into our bed.'

Pretty soon, every night Rebecca just hopped up and got into bed with her Mum and Dad. She didn't care that Mum and Dad didn't want her there. She was *not* going in her own bedroom.

That's the end of the story so far.
The question is: what sort of things could Rebecca have done that would have helped her to be brave? How could she get back into her own bed?

On the next few pages you can read how Rebecca used the 'Good ideas for busting fears' to help her get over her fear and become brave again.

You too can use the 'Good ideas for busting fears' to get yourself back into bed when you have been scared of burglars.

How Rebecca bossed her fear of burglars

1 Rebecca talked to somebody

The next night, Rebecca's Mum sat down after dinner, held Rebecca's hand, looked into her eyes and said 'Rebecca, Daddy and I are very worried about you being scared of burglars. I want you to tell me all about it.'

It wasn't even dark outside. Rebecca wasn't scared of anything, but all of a sudden she started to cry. She cried and cried!

Then she started to take big deep crying breaths and told her Mum the whole story about how her friend at school had told her about the burglar ... and she wanted to protect her Mum and her Dad ... and then it had backfired ... and she had ended up being so scared herself that she had to be *protected* by Mum and Dad.

Her mother just held her and stroked her hair and said, 'It's OK, honey. Thanks for telling me.'

Then she said, 'You go and have a nice bath now'.

While Rebecca was having a bath, Rebecca's Mum rang up her friend's house and had a big talk to her friend's mother.

By the time Rebecca was out of the bath, all warm and snug and cosy and clean, Rebecca's Mum said, 'Rebecca, I want you to ring up Suzy.'

When Rebecca rang Suzy up she could tell Suzy had been crying. 'Why did my Mum tell me to ring you up?' asked Rebecca.

'Well,' said Suzy. 'It's because I told a big fat lie. Rebecca, I never had that scary thing happen to me. There was no burglar. I made it up.'

Well, you could have knocked Rebecca down with a feather. *Suzy had made it up!*

'That was a pretty mean thing to do, Suzy,' she said. 'Why did you do it?'

'Oh, I just wanted to get some attention,' said Suzy. 'I wanted all my friends to listen to me. I'm sorry, Rebecca.'

'Well don't ever do it again,' said Rebecca.

'OK,' said Suzy. 'I'm so sorry.'

Rebecca's Mum looked up at Rebecca and said, 'Do you think you will be all right now, now you know that the burglar wasn't true?'

'Well I'm not sure,' said Rebecca. 'I still feel scared about my own house, even if that burglar didn't come to Suzy's house. There's been burglars for sure at other places. I've seen them taking kids away. It's been in the news and on the TV. How do I know I'm safe?'

'Well,' said Mum, 'we're now going to make a plan! I want you to show me on the fear thermometer how scared you are *before* we make our plan to be brave. Then after you have done the plan, you can show me how *brave* you are then.' (You can see the fear thermometer on page 35.)

Well, Rebecca coloured in up to 10 on the fear thermometer. Guess what it was at the end of doing her plan?

2 She made sure she had a safe and comfortable space around her

Rebecca's Dad then walked in and said, 'Rebecca, take my hand. We're going to check all the windows and all the doors in this house and you can see for yourself that we're very safe, very secure and locked in at night.'

And he did. Rebecca learned that there's a thing called a deadlock. When it's deadlocked nobody can get in or out. All of the windows and all of the doors had a deadlock. That made her feel very much safer at night. Nobody could get in her window. *She* couldn't get out.

3 Rebecca found out the facts

Mum and Dad sat down with Rebecca and gave her a book to read called *Stranger Danger*. This book tells you a lot about strangers and how to handle them so that they don't trick you into going with them.

'Well, that's all right for the daytime,' said Rebecca. 'But what about at night time. I'm sound asleep and they're not tricking me when they're *stealing me* out of my bed.'

'Well, the facts are,' said Mum, 'burglars do sometimes take children, but it's very, very rare and they've never taken a child when there's been a deadlock on the window, and we've got deadlocks, right, Rebecca?'

'Oh, yes, good,' Rebecca said. She was feeling a *bit* safer.

4 Rebecca knew what to expect

Mother said, 'Now there's been lots of scary things on TV lately about kidnapping and about bad robbers. From now on the TV is banned after your favourite TV show. Instead, I want you to go and play for a little while and read a nice story after your bath and then it will be time to go to sleep. I'll come and give you a kiss and cuddle and we will play the 'Goodnight, Sleep Tight Game'.

'Oh, that sounds good,' said Rebecca. She liked the Goodnight, Sleep Tight Game. It was played when her Mum tucked her in at night.

First Rebecca had a turn to say three nice things: one about today, one about tomorrow and one about loving each other. Then her Mum told her three nice things about *her*self!

5 Rebecca got a reward every time she was brave

Dad said, 'Now Rebecca, if you can sleep tight every night for the next seven nights, I'm going to give you a sticker every day and, at the end, if you've got seven stickers, I'll take you to the movies on Saturday night.'

'Oh good,' said Rebecca. 'Can we go and see a show that I want to see?' (Her Dad sometimes saw dumb movies about politics and stuff like that.)

'OK,' said Dad, and he gave Mum a wink.

Rebecca liked these rewards:

▲ Things to have, such as stickers, books and nice things to eat; and

▲ things to do, like choosing a TV show to watch; asking a friend to sleep over; or helping Mum make a cake.

What reward would you like?

6 Rebecca copied people who are brave and (7) talked herself through it

Mum said, 'Now, Rebecca, when I was a little girl I was scared of the dark and this is what I used to do. I used to talk to myself and I used to say things like:

'What do I have to do?
'I have to go to bed all by myself and stay in my bedroom all night all by myself.
'That feels a bit scary.
'I can feel my heart beating.

'But what do I have to remember?
'I have to remember that it's safe.
'The deadlocks are on the window. There's a grownup in the house.
'I need my sleep.'

'Let's act it out,' said Mum. 'Let's imagine that we're going to have to do it and that I'm more scared than you've ever been. Just listen to me.'

Mum acted the whole thing out.

Rebecca laughed because she knew that Mum wasn't really scared any more. It was pretty funny to see her Mum be a real scaredy-cat.

'Now it's your turn,' said Mum.

So Rebecca copied her Mum. She talked to herself all the way through. She found that it was easy to go into her bedroom, even though it was dark outside, and to pretend to lie down and pretend to go to sleep.

'Are you still there?' she called out.

'Yes, I'm just here by the door,' said Mum.

Do you know, Rebecca stayed there for five minutes! Both her parents were *very* proud and so was she!

It's good to keep talking to yourself to make you believe in something you can do, be or have. Grown-ups call it 'positive self-talk' or 'affirmations'.

Rebecca didn't know it, but when she played the pretending game she was doing the Darkness Test. This is where the parent tests out the child by seeing if he or she can stay alone in the dark. Ask Mum or Dad to help you do the Darkness Test. It tells you how to do it on page 34.

8 Rebecca learned to relax

'While you're lying down with your eyes closed,' said Mum, 'I'm going to start playing some special music. It's beautiful music from "The Wizard of Oz". It's the song that Dorothy sings about going over the rainbow.'

'Oh! That's nice,' said Rebecca. 'I love "The Wizard of Oz".' (Rebecca had seen this show twenty times already because they had a video.)

'Now just imagine that you're Dorothy,' said Mum, 'and that you're lying down in the fields of poppies about to go to sleep.

'Remember how Dorothy, the Tin Man, the Scarecrow and the Lion all lay down and nearly went to sleep? They were on their way to the castle of the Wizard of Oz.

'Just imagine that it is your turn to take a little trip to the poppy fields, and you can't help but yawn and stretch, and it feels so good, and even though you have ideas in your mind about things you have to do for school and things that might be happening, it is so easy just to close your eyes and go to sleep.

'Your whole body feels loose and floppy just like a rag doll. You're playing the Floppy Game!'

'Oh, that feels nice,' said Rebecca. 'I could nearly go to sleep, Mum.'

Mum laughed. She was proud of Rebecca.

It's good to relax and imagine that you're in the movies, or thinking of favourite people that you like, or favourite animals and what happens in their lives.

You'll enjoy the 'Relaxation Story' on page 42, too. Ask your Mum or Dad to read it to you.

9 Rebecca imagined facing up to her fear

'Now that you're relaxed,' said Rebecca's Mum, 'it's time to imagine that you are facing up to your fear. Start by getting a picture in your mind of how you are when you very first start to be a little weeny bit scared. When is that, Rebecca?'

'Oh, as soon as I turn off my light,' said Rebecca.

'OK then,' said Mum. 'Now imagine that you've turned off the light and you see a burglar come to the window. Imagine that you get your silver laser rocket-propelled zapper out from under your pillow and you zap that burglar into ten pieces.'

Rebecca scrunched up her nose with glee as, in her imagination, she blew that burglar into a zillion smithereens. She felt great! She opened her eyes and gave Mum a wink.

Mum felt relaxed, too, because she knew that Rebecca would be fine tonight to sleep in her own room by herself.

10 Rebecca read stories about people coping with fear

Children's story books are full of heroes who are brave and do wonderful things, no matter how scared they are. You can learn so much from reading these stories.

Rebecca read all her favourite hero stories, like *The Wizard of Oz* and made a list of her favourite heroes. She did some drawings of them too, and put them up on her bedroom wall.

11 Rebecca got some exercise

When Rebecca's Dad came home, he had organised her a wonderful surprise.

'Hi Rebecca,' he said. 'Go get your swimming costume on. We are going to the heated pool for a night swim.'

'Oh fantastic! Thanks Dad,' said Rebecca. She was very excited. She loved swimming and was very keen to practise jumping in the deep end.

After having a lovely time at the pool, Rebecca felt very tired and snuggled up easily into her own bed. When her Dad tucked her in, her eyes were already closing.

'Goodnight, Darlin',' said Dad. 'Sleep tight and don't let the bed bugs bite, dream about me and think about me, I love you, sweet dreams.'

Well Rebecca did not think about burglars, Dad or anything ... she was too busy sleeping.

Remember to exercise. Tired bodies are fit, healthy and happy. Relax and sleep well!

---

12 Rebecca used drawings to express her fear and be boss of it

Rebecca was very quietly working in her room the next morning. Her mother was quite surprised as it was a lovely sunny day. Rebecca usually enjoyed playing outside on those days.

Her mother asked, 'What are you doing, honey?'

Rebecca answered, 'I'm drawing, Mum. So far I've drawn two pictures of scary burglars. You're just in time to watch what I'd do to them if they tried to get me.'

Rebecca's Mum was startled to see Rebecca start to rip her pictures into tiny pieces, but Rebecca was laughing with glee. She said, 'Take that and that and that, you mean old burglars.'

Finally, when there were just little bits of paper in a pile,

Rebecca picked them up and said, 'Follow me, Mum.' Rebecca went into the bathroom and threw the paper bits into the toilet and loudly flushed it. She looked up and smiled at her Mother.

'That's what I think burglars are good for,' she declared. She was so proud. She had bossed her fear.

As a final test her Mother asked her to draw on the fear thermometer again. You guessed it — it was only 2 out of 10!

And that's how Rebecca was able to learn to be boss of her fear of a burglar getting her or robbing her house.

If you are scared of burglars too, find the Fear-buster Supreme Plan on page 106 and work through your plan to be a fear-buster. You can use Rebecca's ideas or think up new ones of your own!

When your plan works, don't forget to tell everyone who cares about you how proud you are. After all it's a big achievement to have courage and overcome a fear. Take time to celebrate your achievement!

Well done!

SAM'S STORY:

Being scared of the dark ... bogeymen ... ghosts ... and things that go bump in the night

How Sam got to be scared of the thing in the dark

Sam was ten. He was a big boy, his Mum and Dad said. Everyone in his family was excited because they were moving to a new house. Sam was excited too.

The new house was big and old. It had lots of stairs and nooks and crannies and little cubby holes to hide in. When Sam got to the new house he ran around and up and down, having a great time exploring. That night when he went to bed, his Mum tucked him in and he felt great.

Then something woke him up in the middle of the night. He looked out into the hallway. What he could see was the space under the stairs. He got up to go to the toilet and looked over into that space and he saw *something* — *something* which he found very, very scary. The *something* made him scream and run to his parents.

Well, Sam's brain knew that there was *nothing* in the cupboard, *but his feelings didn't*.

He felt scared. His brain wanted to go and help his Mum and Dad by getting dressed and doing everything he needed to in his bedroom ... but his feelings didn't want him to go into that bedroom.

So, just for that day, Mum said that she would do the things in his bedroom for him.

Sam went off to school and forgot all about being scared.

That night after dinner when Mum said, 'Time to get ready for bed.' Sam said, 'No. I'm not going to my bedroom.' He screamed and cried so loudly that Dad said, 'All right, but you're not sleeping in our bedroom.'

Mum and Dad had a big walk-in-wardrobe off their bedroom and they put a fold-up bed in there. Sam slept there

with all the stuffy clothes flapping around his ears. At least he wasn't scared because he could hear his Mum and Dad breathing and talking in their bed.

So every night after that, no matter what Sam's parents said, Sam refused to go and sleep in his own bed. He would go and play in his bedroom during the daytime if he had a friend to play with, but never by himself. He just didn't want to go into his own bedroom any more, because when he was in there by himself he thought that *something* could see him.

What could Sam do to be brave?

How could Sam be boss of bogeymen (and of the dark)?

Sam's plan

Sam's Mum and Dad took him to talk to a lady who was an expert on fears. She knew all about people with fears. She understood that Sam's brain didn't want him to be scared of the bedroom, but that his feelings couldn't help it.

The expert said, 'This is called a phobia. A phobia is when — no matter what anybody else says and no matter how much you know in your brain that there's nothing to be scared of — you are still scared with your feelings.'

'That's what I've got,' said Sam.

'Well,' said the lady, 'let's make a plan. Now the best boss of your feelings is your brain and you have to practise making your brain be the boss.'

She said, 'Let's think of some things that your brain could do that could help you be the boss of being scared.' She explained that Sam had to be the boss. That she could only give him ideas. But he was the one who had to use them and practise them.

If you don't practise being boss of your fear, then your
scared feelings might boss your brain right back!

Ideas to help your brain boss your feelings

The magic ring

Just imagine that you have a magic ring. Every time you put on your magic ring, it changes colour and changes into the kind of beautiful, precious jewel that you want. You could have a red ruby ring, a sparkling diamond ring or a sea-green emerald ring. You could even have a polka dot ring or a star-shaped ring.

This ring is so magical that when you put it on you become invisible. When you're invisible there is nothing that can get you or find you. The magic ring's power is so strong. To make it work all you need to do is just rub it up and down or turn it around on your finger and say a magic word.

Now what magic word could you say? It could be 'Abra-cadabra' or it could be 'McDonalds hamburger'!

Sam's first thought of a magic ring was that he would like an opal, a beautiful coloured stone that is found in the middle of Australia. Sam's Dad had one.

Sam said, 'I'm going to have a magic opal ring and it's going to keep me safe at night.'

The next part of the plan was for Sam to have a whole lot of things to do in his bedroom to keep him busy and to help him feel safe.

Things that he could do were to play the Magic Breathing Game, the Naming Game and the Touching Game and also to listen to his very own Relaxing Story tape. (Ask your parents to teach you these games — they're on pages 36–40.)

Magic breathing

Just in case you can't get to sleep at night, you might like to learn about magic breathing.

Magic breathing is something anybody can do. All they need to do is think about it. Pretty soon they forget they are thinking about it and they are doing it — either asleep or awake — breathing so beautifully that they don't have to think about anything else.

Magic breathing is especially helpful at night if you can't get to sleep or if you have things on your mind because, if your mind is thinking about magic breathing and making the holes on your feet bigger and smaller, bigger and smaller, then you don't need to think about anything else.

Ask your parents to show you how to do magic breathing — it tells you on page 40.

THE POWER OF THE MAGIC RING

I'm scared,
I'm scared,
I'm scared to go to bed.

There's something lurking, lurking,
My brain is overworking,
I'm seeing ghosts and ghouly things,
I think I need my magic ring.

Yes, there! I've made them disappear.
So now there's nothing left to fear.

I'm tired,
I'm tired,
My brain is nearly fried.

It's time to shut my eyes and sleep,
To rest and maybe dream so deep
That when I wake to morning's light,
I'll know I'm safe all through the night.

I'm proud,
And shout aloud,
I DID IT BY MYSELF!
WOW!

Sam bossed his fear

That night Sam did all of the things that the plan had said.

He did magic breathing when he had a bath. It was fun. He imagined that the water was soaking up and squirting out of his head and then coming back down around his toes and squirting up again. He imagined that he was his very own fountain.

When he got into bed he did the Touching Game and the Naming Game. He said, 'I, Sam, am powerful and capable!' He turned his magic ring around. He lay down and went sound asleep.

The next day his Mum and Dad said how proud they were of him and his Mum gave him a gold star sticker.

'Tonight, do you think you could sleep in your own room?' she asked.

'Well, not just yet, Mum,' Sam said.

So she got him to agree that he would go and play in his bedroom just before it got dark. All he needed to do was to practise his plan to be brave.

That night Mum came with Sam and stayed in the bedroom with him for ten minutes, and then they went back to his small bed in the walk-in wardrobe.

He said, 'That's easy, Mum. Tomorrow night I'm going to see if I can stay in my own bedroom. But will you sleep with me?'

Well, Mum didn't want to sleep with him but she said, 'Just for the first night and then what I'm going to do is: I'll stay with you just for a little while and every night I'm going to stay for a shorter and shorter and shorter time. So in the end you're staying there by yourself.'

'OK,' said Sam. 'But what happens if I wake up in the middle of the night and I'm scared?'

'Well,' said Mum, 'what we will do is tie a little piece of string on my finger and a little piece of string on your finger. It will go all the way up the passage, up the stairs and into my bedroom and if you wake up in the middle of the night, scared, all you need to do is just tug on the string and you'll know I'm there.'

'Oh, that's good,' said Sam. 'Then I'll feel safe.'

So on the next night Mum stayed in the room for thirty minutes; on the night after that she stayed for twenty minutes; then ten minutes; and ... on the next night she just tucked him in and left the bedroom.

He felt very safe because he knew that he had the string that he could tug on Mum's finger.

After seven days of that it was his birthday and he was having a friend to sleep over.

'What if my friend trips over the string?' he said to Mum.

'Well, do you think that if your friend is sleeping with you you won't need the string?' asked Mum.

'Sure,' said Sam.

That night Sam didn't need the string because his friend was there. It was so easy. The next night he didn't need the string either.

The very first night that Sam slept in the bedroom all by himself, they all had a special breakfast where Sam chose pancakes and maple syrup, his favourite things.

'I'm not going to be scared of that old cupboard any-more,' he said. And he went and opened it and yelled 'BOO' into it.

Then he stood up and said these amazing words, 'I, Sam, am powerful and capable.' And do you know what ... he was!

And that's how Sam was able to learn to be boss of his fear of the dark and the *something* in the dark.

If you are scared of the dark too, find the Fear-buster Supreme Plan on page 106 and work through your plan to be a rear-buster. You can use Sam's ideas or think up new ones of your own!

When your plan works, don't forget to tell everyone who cares about you how proud you are. After all it's a big achievement to have courage and overcome a fear. Take time to celebrate your achievement!

Well done!

PETER'S STORY:

Being scared of big black dogs

How Peter got scared

Peter loved his big sister. He was 8 and she was 13. Other kids' big sisters used to ignore their little brothers or call them names. Peter's sister Pamela never called him names. She thought up games that they could play together and she took him places.

One thing she liked to do was to go and feed the scraps to the dog next door.

Peter and Pamela didn't have a dog and Pamela loved dogs and wanted to be a dog trainer when she left school.

Peter didn't like the dog next door. His name was Butch. Butch had a big square black and white head and a great big round body with short legs. He always dripped spit down the side of his jaw and his eyes were sometimes red.

Most of the time, Peter would stay on his side of the fence. He would just climb up on the fence and watch Pamela feed Butch.

One day Pamela said, 'You'll have to come with me, I've got so much here and the bowl is too wobbly.' So Peter went through the back garden into Butch's space.

Peter's Dad didn't like Pamela going in to feed Butch because he had heard some people talk about there being a mean dog next door that had once attacked a baby in a pram. But when Peter's Dad spoke to Butch's owner the neighbour said that the mean dog wasn't Butch. Peter's Dad said, 'That owner has a shifty look in his eye. Now, you kids be very careful. He might be telling an untruth.'

'Sure Dad,' said Pamela. 'Look, Butch loves me, Dad, I've got a way with animals. You know that. We will be fine.'

'All right,' said Dad, 'but I don't like it. Be very careful.'

Well, after a couple of nights of feeding Butch, Peter almost started to get used to it. He didn't like how big Butch was and he didn't like the way Butch sometimes looked at him when he went near Pamela. But he liked helping Pamela by carrying the bones.

But one night it happened.

Peter was holding the bones, waiting for Pamela to put the scraps into Butch's bowl, and Peter was looking up at the trees, watching a special kind of bird that he hadn't noticed before.

Suddenly he felt something bite him on the arm. Oh, it did hurt. Peter screamed and dropped the bones.

Pamela looked up to see that Butch had attacked Peter! The dog was biting all up and down Peter's body.

'Stop, Butch, stop!' Pamela yelled. She grabbed the bowl of water and threw it on Butch, but Butch didn't stop biting. She got a stick and started hitting Butch, but he still didn't stop biting.

Then Pamela remembered that she had heard that dogs like Butch wouldn't let go once they started to bite, but the one thing you could do was to hose them with a very sharp hose. So Pamela, being a quick-thinking girl, grabbed the hose and squirted it right in Butch's eyes.

Butch didn't like the hose. Suddenly he let go of Peter and ran up to the corner of the garden.

By this time Peter was on the ground, screaming and screaming, and blood was everywhere. Pamela got him up and together they ran back through the gate and home.

'Mum, Mum, help, help,' Pamela cried.

Mum took Peter to the hospital and he had to have ten stitches in four spots on his body. The doctor said, 'That dog has made a very bad mess here. We are going to have to do plastic surgery on Peter and even then I'm afraid he is going to have bad scars.'

Peter had to have an injection to make sure there was no poison from Butch's teeth that would get into his blood and make him sick. The next thing he knew he was sound asleep in his own bed with bandages all up and down his side. He hoped he would never see Butch again.

And that is exactly what happened. If a dog attacks a kid, then that dog has to be taken away and destroyed. Peter's Dad demanded that Butch be destroyed and even Pamela wasn't sad. She hated what Butch had done to Peter.

Peter had to stay home from school for a whole week and when he went back to school he wore long trousers and a T-shirt even though it was summer.

One day he had to wear bathers when they went swimming. All the other kids looked at him and then started to laugh.

'What are those big lumpy bits on your skin?' they teased.

Peter felt terrible. 'It's scars from a dog attack,' he said.

'Well they just look like lumpy bits to us,' said the kids, and they all laughed.

Peter felt very bad. 'Oh why did I ever go near that dog?' he thought.

From then on Peter would not go near a dog. The family went down to the beach at summer time, but Peter stayed in the holiday house. He would only go to the beach during the day when he was with Mum and Dad and then he stayed very close. There was a sign on the beach that said 'No Dogs Allowed', but people seemed to break the rules by letting their dogs go on the beach at any time.

One day, when Peter was sitting there happily making a sand castle and minding his own business, all of a sudden a dog came running up to him, jumped on his sand castle, sprayed wees in the air and even licked him on the face!

Peter ran screaming to his parents. By now Peter was really scared of dogs — any dogs. He didn't even like seeing dogs on television or in books, and he *definitely* didn't like seeing a dog in real life. Even if it was his best friend's dog and they promised that it wouldn't hurt him, he wasn't going to trust any dog, not after what Butch had done to him.

Pretty soon Peter couldn't go anywhere outside of the house without being scared that he would see a dog. He didn't even like staying in the car when they were at the shops in case a dog came along and jumped up on the car door handle.

It was time to make a plan. The plan was all about how Peter could get used to dogs again.

Can you understand how Peter felt?

Probably you wouldn't want to trust dogs either.
The trouble is:

▲ There *are* always dogs on the beach.

▲ There *are* always dogs on the street.

▲ There *are* dogs at other people's houses when you go to visit.

If you're terrified of dogs, you have to get over your fear because it is very likely that you're going to meet a dog.

How to be boss of dogs when you used to be scared of them

Peter's plan

Peter needed his Mum and Dad's help. They read the Good ideas for busting fears list and chose:

NUMBER 6: Copy people who are brave. People in pictures, photographs, movies and real life.

NUMBER 7: Talk yourself through it.

NUMBER 10: Read lots of stories that show how people and animals cope with their fear.

---

6 Looking at pictures and photographs

The first thing that Peter's Mum did was to go and borrow some books about dogs from the library. She asked Pamela to sit down with Peter and read the dog books.

At first he would only read the ones with cartoons, but gradually he started to look at some of the other ones. At first he would only look at the pictures of little dogs but gradually he started to look at the bigger ones.

Watching movies

Then a movie came to town which was called 'Benji the Hunted'. It was all about a dog called Benji. Pamela asked Mum if she could go to see it. She loved to see animal stories. Peter didn't really want to go but Pamela promised to hold his hand, so he went.

At first he was a bit scared, but Benji was such a little dog, and he was really quite cute and he *was* in the movies. Peter knew that movies were only movies and not real life.

But, the time had come! Now it was time to meet a dog in real life.

One of their friends had a chihuahua (the tiniest dog of all). The chihuahua was called 'Jellybean', because she was black and her owner's favourite jellybeans were the black ones.

Peter took chances to get used to the dog

First chance

At Jellybean's house Peter could hear the dog barking out the back. He said to his Mum, 'I'm not going out there, Mum. I don't care if it is a little dog, I don't want to go outside! It's got sharp teeth and it might jump on me.'

So all Peter would do the first time was look out the window at Jellybean. He felt quite safe behind the glass. He could see that Jellybean did jump around a lot. She had a fluffy toy in the garden and was wrestling with it. Her teeth certainly were sharp.

Second chance

Next time Peter went to Jellybean's house Pamela said, 'Look, you can stay inside the kitchen, but just watch me. I'll show you how tame Jellybean is.'

Pamela went out the back and rolled around on the ground with Jellybean. She even let Jellybean jump on her tummy, nibble her ears, play 'wrestles' with her hair, and ... yuk ... even lick her on the face!

All Peter could think about was how smelly the dog's breath must be and how sharp her teeth must be so close to your face. 'I'm not doing that,' he said. 'I'm staying inside.'

Third chance

Next time they visited the house, Pamela brought her friend, Shannon. Pamela explained that Shannon didn't like dogs either but that Shannon was going to be brave and go and pat Jellybean to show Peter that even though Jellybean jumped up and down she couldn't hurt him.

Pamela said, 'Would you please come outside, Peter, if I promise to hold your hand? If Jellybean comes near you I'll pick her up.'

'All right,' said Peter, but he held Pamela's hand very tight.

They stood just outside the door and Peter watched Shannon go towards Jellybean. Shannon was talking to herself.

'Is she mad?' Peter thought. Then he started to listen. He thought, 'Hey, that makes sense.'

Shannon was talking to herself about not being scared. This is the sort of thing she was saying.

Now what do I have to do? I have to be able to show Peter that I'm not scared of this dog. I remember being jumped on by a big black dog once in the street. Well, this isn't a big black dog, it's only a little dog and what I have to do is just go over and pat it and talk to it, so that it will then let me pick it up and give it a pat.

I'll take a big deep breath and I'll count to ten very, very slowly. One, two, three, four, five, six, seven, eight, nine, ten. That's good. I'm feeling much better now. It's really going to be quite easy.

Shannon walked up to Jellybean, bent down and patted her. Do you know what? It was as if Jellybean knew it was Shannon's first turn at being brave. Jellybean kept very, very still.

'She likes to be patted', said Pamela.

Shannon said, 'That's good. She does feel nice and warm.'

Well before you knew it, Shannon had picked up Jellybean and Jellybean was snuggled very, very still against Shannon's chest.

'She's hardly even a dog,' said Shannon.

Peter thought, 'Yeah, that's what you think.' He could still see those sharp teeth, and why did Jellybean have to have such big googly eyes?

Pamela said, 'Please, Peter, would you see if you could touch Jellybean too?'

Peter said, 'Well, I'll only come near her if Shannon holds her very still, and you help me by holding my hand.'

'All right,' said Pamela. 'Now just talk to yourself the same way that Shannon did.'

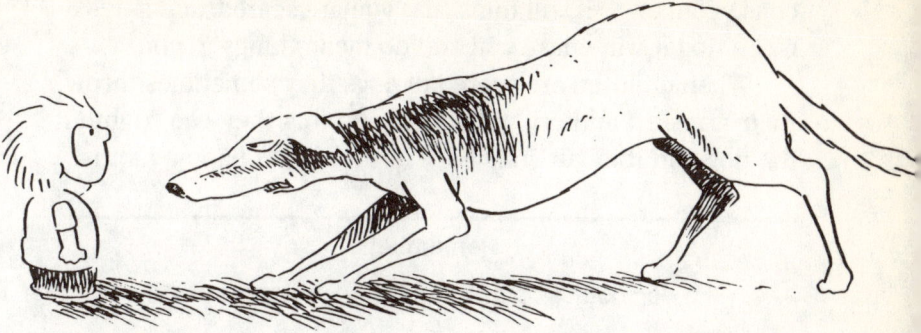

So Peter started to talk to himself and said all the right things, and before you know it ... he found himself standing in front of Jellybean. He put out a hand and very softly and quickly touched the dog's nose and then took his hand away again.

Hooray! He'd done it! He couldn't wait to tell Mum and Dad and he ran inside excitedly, yelling, 'I patted Jellybean! I'm so proud of myself!'

What next?

Well, Peter had overcome his fear of *small* dogs but that didn't mean that he could cope with the great big black dog in the street.

What do you think he should do?

Big black dogs *are* scary and big black dogs *might* do something that you don't want. They might jump on you, or dribble on you, or lick you and they do have smelly breath.

Probably it's very wise to be
careful around big dogs.

Don't run away from dogs

The main thing is that you feel comfortable around little dogs and that you don't have to run away in terror from a big dog. Whenever you run from big dogs you are in danger because the dog will think that you want to play, and it will chase you, or ... it will think that you are scared, and if it is a mean dog it will chase you and do mean things to you.

When children are scared of dogs they sometimes throw their arms up and cry. When they do this they can frighten the dog and it might snap back at the child's flapping arms.

Remember:

▲ If a dog comes up and barks at you, just stand still.

▲ Don't scream suddenly.

▲ Keep your arms down by your sides.

▲ Just stare at it. Stare into its eyes and walk slowly backwards.

Use Peter's ideas

And that's how Peter was able to learn to be boss of his fear of dogs. If you are scared of dogs too, find the Fear-buster Supreme Plan on page 106 and work through your own plan to be a fear-buster. You can use Peter's ideas or think up new ones of your own!

When your plan works, don't forget to tell everyone who cares about you how proud you are. After all, it's a big achievement to have courage and overcome a fear. Take time to celebrate your achievement!

Well done!

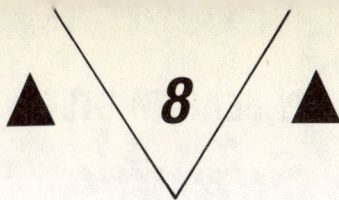

The child's own secret fear-buster plan

Introduction

Well now that you know a lot of good ideas about being brave it's your turn to make your own plan to bust through your fear.

You can use these ideas for *any* fear — it doesn't have to be one we've talked about in the book. Whatever your fear, you can make your own Fear-Buster Supreme Plan!

MY FEAR-BUSTER
Supreme
PLAN

1 **What am I scared of?**
I'm scared of:

_____

2 **What happens now?**
When I'm a **scaredy cat**:
What I do now is:

_____

How I feel now is:

_____

3 **What do I want to happen?**
I'm a **brave lion**:
What I *want* to do is:

_____

How I *want* to feel is:

_____

The problems about my scaredy cat me are:
1 I am *not* the boss of my world.
2
3
4
More?

_____

The good things about being a brave lion me are:

1 I *am* boss of my world.

2

3

4

More?

IN CASE OF
FEAR BREAK
GLASS

FEAR
BUSTER
PLAN

Scary signs and signals.

SCARY SIGNS AND SIGNALS
A kid's checklist

Different people have different signs to show that they are scared. Tick which are your signs.

▲ wrinkles on your forehead ☐

▲ sore neck ☐

▲ sore shoulders ☐

▲ sweaty hands ☐

▲ heart beating faster ☐

▲ face feels hot ☐

▲ shaking hands ☐

▲ tummy feels as if it is full of butterflies ☐

▲ feeling sick ☐

▲ scratching ☐

▲ wiggling your feet up and down ☐

▲ wanting to run away ☐

▲ grinding your teeth ☐

▲ you can't get your words out ☐

▲ feeling as if you'll faint ☐

▲ biting your nails ☐

▲ your stomach feels as if you've stopped in a lift suddenly ☐

▲ feeling dizzy ☐

▲ feeling as if you're going to choke ☐

MY CHECKLIST OF GOOD IDEAS
FOR BUSTING FEARS

To be brave I will:

▲ **Good idea No. 1**
Talk to: _____
_____

▲ **Good idea No. 2**
Make my comfortable and safe space by: _____

_____

▲ **Good idea No. 3**
Know that the truth about fear is: _____

_____

▲ **Good idea No. 4**
I know these things about what to expect and how and
when to do things to cope: _____

_____

_____

▲ **Good idea No. 5**
My rewards will be: _____
Mini rewards on the way to being brave will be:

_____

_____

My final *big* reward for the *big* celebration of when I'm
brave will be:

_____

_____

▲ **Good idea No. 6**
   A brave person I can copy from is:

   _____

   To be brave they are always: _____
   _____

▲ **Good idea No. 7**
   To be brave, all I have to tell myself is:

   _____

▲ **Good idea No. 8**
   My favourite way to relax is: _____
   _____

▲ **Good idea No. 9**
   In my imagination I can bust through my fear by:

   _____
   _____

▲ **Good idea No. 10**
   Stories that show how to be brave with my fear are:

   _____
   _____

▲ **Good idea No. 11**
   My regular exercise programme is:

   _____
   _____
   _____

▲ **Good idea No. 12**
   My drawing of me being brave looks like this:

MY FEAR-BUSTER
Supreme
GAMES PLAN

The ideas and games from this book that I will use to help me bust through my fears are:

1 The Good Night, Sleep Tight Game ☐

2 The Relaxation Story ☐

3 The Magic Ring ☐

4 The Magic Breathing Game ☐

5 The Naming Game ☐

7 The Touching Game ☐

8 The Who Am I? Where Am I? Game ☐

Congratulations!

You are now an expert in understanding, coping with and busting through your fears. As you grow up you can use the 'Good ideas for busting fears' for any worry, upset or fear you might meet along the way. Good luck!

Be brave

Take control of your mind

Make your imagination work for you

Be the boss of your brain

Congratulations

You are now
an official

Fear-buster
SUPREME

▲ *APPENDIX I* ▲

Last word to children

WELCOME!

SPECIAL FEAR-BUSTING SUPREME MEMBERSHIP INVITATION

You can be a member of the:

'I'M BOSS OF MY WORLD' CLUB

To join up, just fill in the membership form, draw a picture and write some sentences about your fear and how you overcame it, using your own plan.

YOU CAN BE A WINNER!

The best fear-buster true stories will receive a special SURPRISE GIFT.

For your annual investment of $25.00 you will get:

▲ A 'fear-buster supreme' badge

▲ A birthday card on your birthday

▲ A newsletter where your story and pictures will be published

Membership application

YES, I want to join the I'M BOSS OF MY WORLD CLUB

Name: _____

Address: _____

_____

_____ Postcode: _____

Birthdate: _____

Amount enclosed: _____

Method of payment: _____

I enclose:

▲ My picture of me being brave

▲ My sentences about my Fear Busting Plan

▲ Anything else? (a story, a poem?)

Parent's signature: _____

▲ *APPENDIX 2* ▲

Last word to parents

Dear Parent,

We would love to have your comments and suggestions on the usefulness of this book. We would like to hear about your experiences with fears, too. Please write to Dr Janet Hall, PO Box 601, Kew, Victoria, Australia 3101.

Audiotapes available

Relaxation audiotapes are available on request. These cover general body/brain co-ordination and relaxation to encourage the listener to relax.

Personalised tapes can be far more effective and can be arranged at special request.

Please write to the following address:

Dr Janet Hall
P.O. Box 601
Kew, Victoria, Australia 3101.

Telephone: (03) 853 3377
Fax: (03) 853 5693

▲ *FURTHER READING* ▲

Biddulph, Steve, *The Secret of Happy Children*, Revised edition, Bay Books, Kensington, NSW, 1988.

Bourgeois, P., & Clark, B., *Franklin in the Dark*, Ashton Scholastic, Gosford, NSW, 1986.

Brett, D., *Annie Stories*, McPhee Gribble/Penguin, Melbourne, 1986.

Diagnostic and Statistical Manual of Mental Disorders (3rd Ed., Rev.) (DSM III), American Psychiatric Association, Washington D.C., 1987.

Dyer, Dr W., *What Do You Really Want for Your Child?*, Bantam Press, Great Britain, 1985.

Gackenbach, D., *Harry and the Terrible Whatzit*, Scholastic Book Services, New York, 1977.

Griffin, M. & Hudson, A. (Eds), *Children's Problems*, Circus Books, Melbourne, 1979.

Hall, Dr J., *Disneyland Dads and Martyred Mums.**

Hall, Dr J., *Fight-Free Families.**

Hall, Dr J., *How You Can Be Boss of Bedtime.**

Hall, J., *How You Can Be Boss of the Bladder*, Janet Hall Pty Ltd, Melbourne, 1989.

Hall, Dr J., *No More Nagging.**

Hazbry, N. & Condy, R., *How to Get Rid of Bad Dreams*, Scholastic-TAB Publications, Ontario, 1983.

Hill, S., *One Night at a Time*, Fontana Picture Lions, London, 1984.

Irvine, J., *Coping with Kids*, Horwitz Grahame, Sydney, 1988.

Irvine, J., Irvine, W. & Wallace, I., *Coping with School*, Simon & Schuster, Sydney, 1992.

Jacobs, N., *Toddlers, Teens and Inbetweens*, Smarkprint, Bendigo, 1989.

King, N. J., Hamilton, D. I. & Ollendick, T. H., *Children's Phobias: A Behavioural Perspective*, John Wiley & Sons, New York, 1988.

Koda-Callan, E., *The Magic Locket*, Workman Publishing Co., New York, 1988.

McKinnon, P., *Quiet Magic*, David Lovell Publishing, Melbourne, 1990.

Palmer, P., *Liking Myself*, Impact Press, California, 1977.

Palmer, P., *The Mouse, the Monster and Me*, Impact Press, California, 1977.

Remsberg, B. & Saunders, A., *Help Your Child Cope with Stress*, Piatkus, England, 1986.

Sarafino, E. P., *The Fears of Childhood: A Guide to Recognizing and Reducing Fearful States in Children*, Human Sciences Press, New York, 1986.

Saunders, A. & Remsberg, B., *The Stress Proof Child: A Loving Parent's Guide*, Cygnet, New York, 1986.

Young, B., *Stress in Children, How to Recognise, Avoid and Overcome It*, Nelson, Australia, 1986.

Zimbardo, P. G., *The Shy Child*, McGraw Hill, New York, 1982.

*Pre-publication editions of these books are available from Dr Janet Hall, P.O. Box 601, KEW, VIC, 3101, Melbourne, Australia.

▲ INDEX ▲